A Canadian Challenge
Le défi québécois

CHRISTIAN DUFOUR

A Canadian Challenge
Le défi québécois

CHRISTIAN DUFOUR

 co-published by
Oolichan Books
and
The Institute for Research on Public Policy
L'Institut de recherches politiques

1990

Reprinted 1991

ISBN 0-88982-105-4 (Oolichan)
ISBN 0-88645-113-2 (I.R.P.P.)

Canadian Cataloguing in Publication Data
Dufour, Christian, 1949-
    A Canadian challenge — Le défi québécois

    In Engish only.
    Translation of : Le défi québécois.
    Co-published by: Institute for Research on Public Policy.
    Includes bibliographical references.
    ISBN 0-88982-105-4 (Oolichan). --ISBN 0-88645-113-2 (IRPP)

    1. Quebec (Province) -- History. 2. Nationalism --Quebec (Province) 3. Canada --English-French relations. 4. Canada--Politics and government--1984-
I. Institute for Research on Public Policy. II. Title. III. Title: Le défi québécois.
FC2920.I28D8313 1990   971.4   C90-091532-3
F1053.2.D8313 1990

First Published in Canada in French by
Éditions de l' HEXAGONE, 900 rue Ontario est,
Montréal, Québec H2L 1P4

Cover Illustration: Nicholas Letarte

Published by
Oolichan Books
Lantzville, B.C., Canada V0R 2H0

and

The Institute for Research on Public Policy/
L' Institut de recherches politiques
P.O. Box 3670 South
Halifax, Nova Scotia, Canada B3J 3K6

Printed and bound in Canada by
Hignell Printing Limited, Winnipeg, Manitoba

À Gilles.

TABLE OF CONTENTS

FOREWORD

The publication of Christian Dufour's essay *Le défi québécois* was a major literary event in Quebec in the fall of 1989. The prestigious *L'Actualité*, under the headline "Un Québec fort dans un Canada uni," introduced a key extract as follows: "En primeur: un extrait d'un nouveau livre qui analyse avec une rare finesse les contradictions de l'identité québécoise." It predicted, accurately, that everyone would be talking about Dufour's work ... and the Quebec media continued to discuss the work through the Spring of 1990.

The discussion is not confined to French-language media. Gretta Chambers, of the Montreal *Gazette*, said it is "a book all Canadians should read, as much for the story of how we got here as for its insights into our present state." Charles Taylor observed, in a review for *Compass* of "this exceptionally insightful book," that "perhaps it would be a better course ... somehow to find a Canada where we could be what we are. Or is it too late? These are questions that Dufour makes us face."

The Institute agrees with the need to introduce Dufour's questions into the public debate of issues which include, but have a much larger compass than, the Meech Lake Accord. It has therefore arranged to co-publish with Oolichan Books this translation of Dufour's work, which was itself the fruit of two year's research and reflection during his secondment from the Quebec Government to the Institute.

An extract, in translation, has already been published in the December 1989 issue of *Policy Options*, under the title of *The Quebec Challenge*. This literal translation of the French title captures, however, only a part of the message of Dufour's book. The Quebec Challenge is, in fact, a challenge to all Canada.

"What is English Canada?" asks the author. He concludes that, whereas Quebec has at least in part come to terms with its own unique identity, English Canada has not successfully defined itself. Without such definition, Dufour argues, Canada is incapable of resolving the place of a confidently different Quebec within an optimistic and united Canada—(or indeed, in my view, of resolving its wider problems as a multicultural nation with an aboriginal heritage.) Although English Canada is prepared, probably, to grant that Quebec is different, it is not prepared to accept frankly the political consequences of that fact. Without such an acceptance, the country faces a future of perpetual squabbling—or the separation of Quebec.

This is not a "separatist" book. Dufour argues that, at least until now, the Anciens Canadiens and their descendants have fared better in first the British and later the Canadian surroundings than they would have done alone. He points to the assimilation of the army of emigrants to New England as a caution to those francophones who see only the positive side of independence. Both Canada and Quebec, it seems clear to me, have far more to gain by staying together than by moving apart. But in any case, Dufour concludes, the present relationship, still based essentially on the Conquest of 1763, must be fundamentally changed.

The Institute's efforts to improve public understanding of these issues, which have now exacerbated to crisis proportions, began almost with its 1972 birth. From *La situation demolinguistique au Canada: évolution passée et prospective* (Rejean Lachapelle and Jacques Henripin) to Malone's *Une place pour le Québec au Canada,* they have covered economic, social, and cultural aspects of the Canadian dilemma. Nor have Institute publications been limited to Canada-Quebec or English-French questions. The Institute recognizes, as does Dufour, that the Atlantic and the West have their own problems and feel their own forms of alienation within this geographically vast country. Gordon Robertson, a former President of the Institute, reflected the West's concerns in particular when he wrote *A House Divided,* published by the Institute shortly after *Le défi québécois* appeared last fall.

Evidently it is time to look beyond the debate over the Meech Lake Accord. The experience of that debate is not reversible, least of all in Quebec. Attitudes have changed dramatically, and some social decisions have, in effect, been taken. Federal-provincial relations cannot now return to "business as usual" within the existing structures.

What is needed instead is to recapture some of the reasoned

approaches, based on the underlying goodwill which still characterizes this country, outlined by observers like Dufour and Robertson, while searching for the new federal frameworks needed to accommodate the new realities of Canadian life in the emerging global information society.

This publication itself is a happy reflection of the ability of Canadians to work together. The Institute has had excellent relations with Alain Horic, of l'Hexagone, which published the original work in French in Montreal. His agreement with Oolichan Books, for a joint IRPP-Oolichan publication in English, has created something of a Vancouver Island-Montreal "axis." Christian Dufour adds his Quebec City extension to the axis and has worked closely with translator Heather Parker, a Nova Scotia resident with a degree in translation from Laval University. Jeffrey Holmes, of the IRPP's Ottawa office, has acted as translation editor and co-ordinator of these trans-Canada efforts. The result, we trust, illustrates in a small way the reservoir of goodwill and the foundation of working relationships on which Canadians can still build a nation in which distance and diversity are strengths rather than handicaps.

A renewed Canadian community, full of promise as it enters a new century, is possible. But reaching it now will demand some fundamental changes in our structures of governance, in an extraordinary exercise of social will. The possibilities for patchwork are past, and, like Canadian governments themselves, the Institute's continuing work in this field must search more deeply for the principles of a new federal framework.

This book provides a foundation and a starting point for the search.

Rod Dobell
June 1990

PREFACE

The Origins of this book are personal . I was born in 1949, so I have no real memories of political life before the Quiet Revolution. I am also from Saguenay-Lac-Saint-Jean, one of the most francophone regions of Quebec, colonized during the last century in response to the exodus of French Canadians to the United States. One of my brothers used to say: "When I was five or six, I found out there were people who didn't speak French. I was astonished. Later, when I realised that there were more English people in Canada than French, I was completely thrown." Coming from that generation and that region, it is difficult to be a nationalist and sensitive to the concept of Quebec power.

I worked in the field of federal provincial relations for the Quebec government from 1975 to 1987. The self destructive side of Quebecers' political action seemed to me to be clearly reflected by what happened between 1965 and 1982: a constitutional revision, set in motion as a response to Quebec's historical dissatisfaction, resulted in a weakening of the province, mainly because of the Quebecers' own actions. English Canadians looked on. The only institutional power controlled by Francophones is diminishing—too often due to francophone actions.

The research which led to this book was carried out under the aegis of the Institute for Research on Public Policy (IRPP). This was deliberate. With a board that includes federal and provincial representatives, the IRPP reflects somewhat the image of Canada. Formally bilingual, in accord with the Trudeau ideal, the organization has few contacts with the Quebec that came out of the sixties.

This essay is marginal in comparison to works usually sponsored by the IRPP, especially because of its personal nature. One of the Institute's great merits was its acceptance of a project that was, in a number of ways, foreign ... as Quebec still is within Canada.

A very special thanks to the IRPP's Director of Communications, Mr. Jeffery Holmes, without whom this book wouldn't have been published in English.

Change what can be changed, accept what cannot be changed and, above all, know how to tell the difference.

But that does not stop the pain when faced with something that cannot be changed, yet should be. That does not stop the regrets.

INTRODUCTION

This book deals with the Conquest of 1763, the Rebellion of 1837, and many other historical events, especially in the following chapter. But it isn't a history book. It is a political essay on contemporary Quebec and Canada. To prepare for the future, and modify outdated but deeply rooted reactions, it's useful to understand why such reactions came to be. That is one way to avoid both the illusion of change and change for the worse.

It is increasingly apparent that Quebec is poorly integrated in the Canadian framework. This is particularly true since the December 1988 Supreme Court decision on the language of commercial signs. The events of the past twenty-five years have aggravated a potentially dangerous situation. While the British North America Act of 1867 was content to ignore, virtually, the French-Canadian nationalism of the times, since 1982 Quebec society has been at odds with a constitution-alized vision of Canada that is not compatible with its own reality. In the worst-case scenario, we risk sinking into an inextricable situation, such as the one in Northern Ireland.

This essay attempts to describe two parameters, which some would believe irreconcilable. As regards the first, Canada is profoundly dependent on the conquest of 1763, and its appropriation of the political consequences that flow spontaneously from Quebec's specificity. This becomes even more apparent when Quebec, the old Canadian Nation of Patriots and originally the only true nation in the country, is incapable of getting itself recognized as a modestly distinct society within Canada. The other parameter is that, within the geopolitical context of North America, it is to Quebec's advantage to have a politically functional

Canada. Within the realm of the possible, it is better for Francophones to be inside rather than outside Canada.

In this book, I shall often speak of "Quebec identity" and "Canadian identity," rather than of "the Quebecer" or "the Canadian." This is to reflect the fact that, in Quebec, the two identities are often entangled within the same person. Because this concept includes structuring elements that were determinant in the formation of these identities, it also allows us to take an in-depth view of history. Even though Quebecers and Canadians often overlook these elements, they are nonetheless present in their collective subconscious. It is important not to confuse "Quebec identity," as used in this sense, with the sporadic perception that the Quebec people may have of themselves. The movement of waves on an ocean's surface is not a reliable indication of the strength of the current in the depths.

The study of the formation of the Quebec and Canadian identities also allows us to use some psychological concepts. This is useful because the national phenomenon is largely psychological in nature. In this respect, this essay is but a foray into a broad field still to be explored. For Quebecers are still very much affected by the aftermath of the abandonment/conquest they experienced in the 18th century, which remains buried in their collective subconscious.

The French motherland's abandonment of Canada and the British conquest came at the end of a long and terrible war. Quebec's developing identity would be forever scarred by it. The original trauma was almost immediately pushed into the back of the Anciens Canadiens' collective subconscious because they did not have a bourgeoisie strong enough to cope with the event on a political plane. Besides, their state of shock made the conquered people very sensitive to the exemplary behaviour of the British during the military occupation between the defeat of 1759-1760 and the Conquest proper.

In 1764, after the Conqueror had put in place an oppressive civil administration, some of the British found it in their interests to stand up for the Anciens Canadiens, whose power of entrenchment and seduction was considerable. These British helped bring about the adoption, in 1774, of a Quebec Act that recognized the essential national rights of the Anciens Canadiens.

De facto, some of the British served partially as the elite for Quebecers' ancestors at a crucial time in the development of the collective identity. The suppressed trauma, however, would later render the new elite (which would develop after the 1790s) politically unrealistic and idealistic. This state of affairs had much to do with the failure of the Patriot Rebellion of 1837-38.

It also has a lot to do with the Quebec problem—the Canadian problem—of today. It's like a neurosis that makes an individual yearn intensely for several incompatible things at the same time. This is demonstrated by Quebecers' tendency not to be collectively realistic in politics. They have difficulty promoting solutions that correspond to their objective situation and long-term interests. This reality has long been obscured by a series of Quebecers who have reaped personal political success. They have wasted too much energy in fighting each other—a recent example being the antagonism between Pierre Elliot Trudeau and René Lévesque.

The merger of the two opposites that have always existed in Quebec, as in other societies, does not come easily. Internally, there is a need to organize a French society; externally, there is a need to participate in the whole of Canada and North America. The first trend extends from Intendant Talon, through the Quiet Revolution of Jean Lesage, and on to the *Parti Québécois*. The second is illustrated by the *coureurs de bois* of New France, who explored the continent, and by the Cartiers, Lauriers, and Trudeaus.

When Quebecers follow one or the other of the two trends, they demonstrate an idealism that precludes a productive merger between the two tendencies. As a consequence, Canada has been changed over the past few years as a result of Quebecers' actions on the federal scene. These changes were constitutionalized in 1982. Quebec society itself has undergone a mutation since the Quiet Revolution, and the symbol of this transformation is the Charter of the French Language. These two dynamics are fundamentally opposed: Mr. Trudeau's ideal of a bilingual Canada is incompatible with the French Quebec ideal of Bill 101.

This is no longer an exclusively Quebec problem, but a phenomenon that affects all of Canada. The country would have to confront the pernicious consequences of its idealism, even if Quebec were to secede. A growing number of Quebecers and, probably, English Canadians, are dreaming of Quebec's independence. It is understandable that they want to put an end to a problem that continues to worsen.

Until now, the English-Canadian political elites have remained mostly spectators. To resolve a problem they have always had difficulty understanding, or that they did not want to understand, they relied on those Quebecers whose first loyalty was to Canada. Historically, English Canada was the big benefactor of the Conquest. In a country built on this event, the first reaction is often to deny even the existence of the Quebec problem. Lack of interest or denial is becoming more and more pronounced, while the problem becomes more thorny and more Canadian than ever.

As a result of the efforts of principally Quebec players, Canada now displays a more Cartesian image: formally independent of Great Britain, it is bilingual and multicultural, with ten provinces equal in status and citizens protected by a Constitutional Charter of Rights. But the country has lost in flexibility what it has won in coherence. This beautiful structure is not efficient in regard to the two problems that confront the country internally: Quebec nationalism and regional alienation, especially in the West. The system's provincialism[1], accentuated by the refusal to recognize the political consequences of Quebec's specificity, has now attained unprecedented heights. This prevents regional problems from being expressed in productive fashion.

The Canadian identity—if it does not more adequately integrate its dynamic Quebec and regional entities—is too fragile to accept the challenge of a rendezvous with its American neighbour. The decrepitude of the Canadian political structure makes dangerous a Canadian-American economic integration that can only have considerable political consequences.

To confront the problem, we need a clear vision and leadership qualities that English-Canadian political men and women seem incapable of demonstrating. But this lack of vision and leadership doesn't excuse Quebec from the need to exorcise some of the demons that have haunted it for more than two centuries and that mortgage its future, whatever that future may be.

CHAPTER I

A Little History

A young child, abandoned by his parents, was adopted by others. The situation didn't appear to bother him; he even seemed happy about it. He quickly became attached to his foster parents, who loved him. His new mother, especially, had a lot of affection for him, even if his new father couldn't help feeling, at times, that the child was different from the rest of the family.

It seems as if the child has forgotten everything. And he really has.

The adult carries within him the wound of the drama lived in silence by that despairing child.

Under the French regime, New France was already known as Canada, the inhabitants as Canadians. That was the only name for Quebecers' ancestors until the Union of 1840. The others called themselves "the British." The term "Canadiens" is used in this sense in the chapter which follows. In subsequent chapters, these people will be known as the "Anciens Canadiens."

THE UNTHINKABLE

Today, the only event that most Quebecers still remember about the English Conquest of New France is the battle of the Plains of Abraham. There has been a recent tendency to consider it a mere skirmish, rather than something of real importance, probably because of the small number of soldiers involved and the fact that the matter was settled in less than half an hour.

And yet, Wolfe's victory over Montcalm on September 13, 1759, on a plateau overlooking the Saint Lawrence where Quebec stands, is mentioned in every respectable book of world history. To the shrewd observer, that battle was the first clear signal that world hegemony was passing from France to England and that America would be Anglo-Saxon. In this sense, the battle of the Plains of Abraham is more important than the formidable defeat—in all its noise, fury, and glory—of Napoleon at Waterloo, fifty-six years later.

We usually remember the Plains of Abraham, but almost everyone has forgotten that this battle, and the Conquest of New France in general, came after a long and terrible war, by far the most trying that has ever taken place on Quebec or Canadian soil. In September 1760, the winners were faced with a prostrate people. The losers were really a pitiful sight. This fact is not irrelevant to what follows.

New France, during the war, had lost one-seventh of its estimated 1765 population of sixty-five thousand, according to Lionel Groulx. The countryside had been devastated. The British army had torched, systematically, every village from Quebec down both sides of the St. Lawrence, to Baie Saint-Paul on the North Bank and the River Ouelle on the South. After two months of siege and bombardment, only one house remained standing in Lower Quebec City. The majority of the "Habitants" had been under arms for several years. Those who were not had sought refuge in the surrounding woods during the last days of the invasion. The war brought misery and, at its close, famine.

And there was fear, nourished by French and English propaganda. Wolfe's famous proclamation of June 27, 1759, gave enough food for the imagination: "If, to the contrary, misplaced stubbornness and careless valour cause them to take up arms, they (the Canadiens) can expect to suffer the most cruel effects that war has to offer… if they are comfortable in imagining the excesses of fury of which an unleashed soldiery is capable."

French propaganda had had no difficulty convincing the Canadiens of what they risked if the English won: at best, they would be deported, at worst, summarily executed. The Deportation of the Acadians, one of the dishonourable chapters in English colonial history, had just taken place, at the beginning of this war, and was still fresh in their minds. Some of the unfortunate deportees had fled to Quebec, which could not help but spread doubt about the magnanimity of eventual English conquerors. We must keep in mind that we look at the England of 1760 in the light of the evolution of that country, and the West in general, to a higher level of tolerance. For the Canadiens, the British were the hereditary enemy (with all that implies of hatred and fear).

Between the surrender of Quebec City and Montreal, France sent notice that it would suspend redemption of the paper money which the Canadiens had been forced to accept for many years. This was practical confirmation that the motherland had truly abandoned the Canadiens. (She had not sent any ships since 1758.) It was an end of the regime worthy of the colony's scandalous wartime administration under the infamous Intendant Bigot. As a final stroke of bad luck, between the two capitulations the abandoned Canadiens lost their last natural leader. The last Bishop of New France, Mgr. de Pontbriand, died May 8, 1760.

The people really touched bottom during the surrender of Quebec City in September 1759, and of Montreal a year later. In a country where each colonist still had his own gun, the disarmament of the Habitants, during ceremonies which brought together many parishes, was an emotion-filled event. Everyone was involved: highly symbolic, the act was lived as a disgrace. The people were "disarmed" in every sense of the word. Defenseless. Vulnerable.

The worst—military occupation—was yet to come.

But while Montreal was still French, Quebec was already under English rule. And the people began to breathe more easily—there had been, at least thus far, no summary executions.

*

From the surrender of Montreal in September 1760 to the entering into office of the first English civil governor, James Murray, in August 1764, the colony was occupied by the British Army: the country was under martial law. The Conquest was not yet a *fait accompli* and the war between England and France continued elsewhere. Quebec was no longer under the French regime, but not yet under the English.

These four years would be crucial. They would permanently mark the young, developing Canadien identity. It is difficult to understand the problems faced by the Quebec and Canada of today if we do not take into account what happened during that period. While the Canadiens were in a state of shock and entering a phase that should normally have been the most devastating, the behaviour of the British military proved to be correct. Even exemplary.

Michel Brunet, a Quebec historian unlikely to be accused of compliancy on this topic, writes that "the generosity of the Conqueror, his kindness, care for the general interest and his spirit of justice won the hearts of the vanquished [2]." Not only were the Canadiens free from any kind of physical threat, it quickly became clear that there would be no question of deportation. To the contrary: there was some fear that the Canadiens would emigrate, as the Treaty of Paris would give them the right to do in 1763.

The occupiers vied in intelligence and kindness during this period when it was not yet known whether England would keep Canada. The basic characteristics of the French Regime were preserved. The judicial system was still divided into three administrative regions: Quebec City, Trois-Rivières, and Montreal. When the English made changes, it was generally for the better, like paying cash for army purchases. During this time of shortages, and to avoid speculation, the military governors wisely fixed the price of staples such as meat and bread.

At times, the occupiers even proved gentle and considerate. Approximately £8000 were gathered from the English officers to help the most needy of the Canadiens, and soldiers were ordered to salute religious processions in the streets. The Canadiens expected Attila: they got Caesar Augustus. Twenty years after the "Please fire first, Gentlemen of England!" of the Battle of Fontenoy, the spirit was that of a petticoat war.

The Canadiens were deeply touched. This is a delicate subject that embarrasses some historians, but the facts are incontestable. During that period, the Canadiens were more or less seduced by their conquerors. The historian Burt's expression for this period implies something terrible: "the moral conquest."

Numerous examples, not always from the occupiers themselves, are proof of a feeling of content among Quebecers' ancestors. In 1763, the captains of the militia, or what remained of the military elite of New France, sent the governor nothing less than an "affectionate address." The next year, another address was ended with this seemingly unbelievable closing: "Duty is enjoyable when accompanied by affection.[3]" Finally, and as incontestable proof, were the forthcoming marriages of Canadian women to British soldiers.

Seduction would be reciprocal, to a certain degree. The military governor of the Quebec region, James Murray, pitied the vanquished. Four months after the fall of Montreal he wrote to Amherst, his Commander-in-Chief, concerning the miserable situation of the Canadiens: "... to describe it is really beyond my powers and to think of it is shocking to humanity[4]." He preferred these Canadiens to the few dozen English adventurers who followed the British armies and settled almost immediately in Quebec and Montreal.

Murray was to have an important influence on the Canadian identity. It is important, therefore, to take a look at his personality. Brigadier James Murray, the son of Lord Elibank, came from a good Scottish family. Some have said that he was a little like Wolfe, the victor of the Plains of Abraham. Authoritarian but fair, intelligent, muddle-headed, and impetuous, Murray was the product of the old England, aristocratic and rural. As a soldier, he fought fiercely against the Canadiens during the war. (His army ravaged the islands of Sorel and their surrounding region during the summer of 1759.) As a victor he was moved by the distress of those he had conquered.

At first, Murray found the Canadiens ignorant, dominated by their seigneurs and priests. But a military governor about to manage an occupied country appreciated their docility. With time, the gentleman would be seduced by their good manners, reminder still of Old France. In a petition to the English Minister for the Colonies, he described them as "perhaps the best and bravest race on this globe"; later, he "would speak of them as a people he loved and admired.[5]"

Such turgid descriptions would not prevent Murray from thinking that the assimilation of the Canadiens would not only be unavoidable, but desirable, and for their own good. But the military governor of Quebec was somewhat disgusted with the evolution of the English society of his time. This society was losing respect for the aristocratic and military values he so cherished. In England, the pragmatic, mercantile spirit which prevailed was on its way to making the small island off Europe mistress of the world.

The governor found he had affinities and community of interest with a society that had always been militarized and that kept its feudal ways. In 1762 he gave the name Beauport to the property he purchased in England, with the intention of retiring there after his service. He later decided to spend his last days as a seigneur in Canada. He would devote a great deal of money and energy to his seigneury of Lauzon, near Quebec City, when the colony's English merchants succeeded in having him recalled to England.

In retrospect, this uncommon "love story" between the defeated and the occupiers is not that surprising on the Canadian side. After fearing for one's life in a terrible war, and while still in a state of shock after the defeat by the hereditary enemy, and with the increasing signs of France's disregard, surrendering to such kind English people was not merely the only possible objective outcome but it must have been experienced with relief. Almost like a liberation. The Church, the only Canadian elite still politically functional, in spite of the death of the Bishop, had sent its flock an unmistakable message. Even before peace had been officially declared between France and England, a solemn *Te Deum* was sung in the churches in honour of the English victory.

This is analogous to hostages who fall in love with their abductors, when these reveal themselves as captivating individuals. But no comparison is perfect, for the English were far more imposing than vulgar kidnappers. They were the Conquerors.

During the latter days of military occupation, London and Paris had already agreed on the colony's destiny. This was sealed in February 1763 by the Treaty of Paris, which put an end to the Seven Years' War. Canada's abandonment by France was confirmed. In the months that followed, the Board of Trade, the English department responsible for administration of the colonies, drafted in London the Royal Proclamation. This would give what used to be New France its first civil government under the English regime.

The Canadiens did not yet know it, but they were about to be officially abandoned by France and conquered by England. They and their descendants would take some time to grasp fully what had happened.

*

It is clear that what did happen during this period was as much France's abandonment of its colony as it was England's conquest. If France had wanted Canada, it would have been able to keep the country during the signing of the Treaty of Paris, in the context of negotiations concerning not only Europe, but India and the West Indies as well. But France, obviously, didn't want Canada. First and foremost a European power, it had invested a great deal less in New France than had England in its American colonies. While one Englishman in six lived in the New World in 1760, the ratio for the French was only one in three hundred[6].

The historian Mason Wade noted that French Canadians used to call the Conquest the Cession. This was probably to take into account the aspect of the event that had particularly hurt them and that reflected on France's honour: its only inhabited colony, the only part of itself that had started to take root elsewhere, was yielded freely and without regret to the hereditary enemy[7].

The young Canadien identity had as yet no existence independent of France. Understandably so, that identity would be deeply marked or bruised by this desertion, which would be emotionally perceived as rejection. That experience would certainly tarnish the image Canadiens would develop of themselves. It probably explains the traditional francophobia of Quebec's "little" people, which has always contrasted with the love of France of some of the elite.

There was never a serious plan for reconquest. In France, Canada was quickly forgotten. During the American War of Independence, the chivalrous Marquis de Lafayette dreamed of a Franco-American expedition to free Quebec, but the affair was never seriously considered in Versailles. When Alexis de Tocqueville visited Canada in 1831, he expressed his astonishment at finding a French nation completely unknown to Paris. There, those who knew their history thought that the Canadiens had been assimilated.

It was not until De Gaulle's "Vive le Québec libre" in 1967 that an emotional link between the motherland and its old colony was really re-established politically. With his extensive knowledge of French history, the great man felt that he was settling part of "Louis XV's debt," according to his biographer Jean Lacouture. Because of the unique way in which he represented his country, and because of the era, which was still open to this kind of effusion, De Gaulle was the last Frenchman in a position of authority to be able to say to the Canadiens' descendants: France is sorry, France recognizes you as French, France loves you … Most of the message was heard, to the great displeasure of the English Canadians, who reacted bitterly to the outburst. The Quebecois identity emerged stronger than before.

But the reality of 1763 was abandonment, rejection. This transforms a defeat, which you can always hope to reverse, into something permanent: a 'conquest.' Without France's support, it was totally unrealistic for the sixty-five thousand Canadiens to hope to liberate themselves from England, the greatest world power. But being abandoned made the Conquest easier to accept at the time.

There was no choice; even France was in favour of it. Later, when the motherland was swept by atheist revolution, the Canadiens even managed to convince themselves that, all things considered, this was a blessing from heaven.

People are often very surprised that Quebecers say they are still affected by an event that took place over two hundred years ago, while other peoples have already overcome more recent, more devastating defeats. They forget the fundamental difference between defeat and conquest. A conquest is a permanent defeat, an institutionalized defeat.

In 1760, France suffered a major, humiliating defeat by England. She had her revenge fifteen years later, giving the Americans, in their War of Independence against the English, the support that proved the deciding factor. The Canadiens were not really defeated during the Seven Years' War: in general, they had won the battles for which they were responsible[8]. The Canadiens were conquered in 1760.

In accordance with international law of the times, England acquired, in principle, limitless power over them. That is the ultimate catastrophe for a people: being taken over, totally and permanently, by the hereditary enemy. Contrary to the vanquished, the conquered is affected at the heart of his collective identity. He becomes the conqueror's creature, to do with what he may. That the conqueror is magnanimous changes nothing in this reality. On the contrary, it makes the conquest more humiliating because the conquered also has to be grateful.

But these are only concepts—juridical terms. Merely words. A conquest is lived. As Kenneth McRae, a critical observer of Quebec nationalism, wrote in 1964, "To the Canadiens, it was a cataclysm beyond the power of the mind to grasp.⁹" Literally, the unthinkable.

THE FRENCH PARTY

In October 1763 England adopted the Royal Proclamation, giving the colony its first civil government under the English regime. This became effective in August 1764. After the euphoria of the military occupation, it was a brutal awakening for the Canadiens to find themselves under a regime that was tyrannical in principle.

The first rule they learned was that only English law would be recognized. The conquered people were also deprived of any political rights. Unless they renounced Catholicism, which was obviously unthinkable at that time, they could not hold official positions or be publicly employed. Instructions from English authorities, in December 1763, clearly warned the governor not to permit Rome to nominate a new bishop.

The Proclamation also foresaw the earliest possible convocation of a House of Assembly, so that the inhabitants of Canada would not be deprived of the advantages of English democracy. Obviously, the problem was that the sixty-five thousand Canadiens would be excluded from the House; it would be restricted to representing the two or three hundred English merchants now established in the colony.

The intentions of the new metropolis in regard to the Canadiens, already clear in the Proclamation, were detailed in the act nominating Murray as governor and in the instructions he would receive from London. The French colony must be transformed into an English one. It would have to prepare for the arrival of Anglo-Saxon immigrants from Europe and the American colonies. The necessary steps would have to be taken to bring the Canadiens gradually to convert to Protestantism.

The Canadiens became more or less outlaws in their own country. They would now be known, in all seriousness, as His Majesty's new subjects. The *old* subjects were the British merchants who had just arrived.

England was showing its conqueror side.

But for four years the Canadiens had also seen the other side. The paradox of the situation was that England was, at the same time, the conqueror (with all that implies about oppression) and the most politically advanced nation of its time—the model cited by the French philosophers of the Age of Enlightenment. In England, Lord Mansfield would soon write to Prime Minister George Grenville to protest the Royal Proclamation: "The history of the world don't furnish an instance of so rash and injust an act by any conqueror whatsoever.[10]"

But the Royal Proclamation was contested, above all and very effectively, in Canada itself. The administrator of the Quebec region during military occupation, James Murray, had been named the first civil governor of the colony. He, therefore, was the one with the responsibility to apply the repressive Proclamation. It quickly became clear that he would put aside the document's most unjust provisions.

Under the pretext that many articles were obscure or contradictory, and convinced of their unfairness, Murray almost immediately exceeded his powers by reorganizing the administration of justice. Canadiens could serve on the jury of the King's Bench and Canadian lawyers plead before the lower courts. This was September 1764. The Proclamation had been in effect for only one month.

That was the beginning of a series of moves by Murray and his successors; they would eventually make inoperable the provisions of the Proclamation most inimical towards the Canadiens. After threatening to resign, the governor obtained an agreement in June, 1765, that the anti-Catholic provisions of the English Penal Code would be declared nonapplicable to Canadiens. In 1767, the Canadiens' laws of land tenure were confirmed. Such changes would continue until the proclamation of the Quebec Act of 1774, a large part of which would simply be an official recognition of practices that were formerly illegal.

Murray would also refuse to summon the House of Assembly, even though it had been planned for in the Proclamation. It would have been unjust if Canadiens were not represented, and dangerous if the Canadiens were in control—in a word it was premature. In any case, the Canadiens did not want it. As during the military occupation, the watchword was paternalism.

The govenor's refusal to summon the House of Assembly aroused the fury of the British merchants. War was declared—a war that proved fierce. Murray could not find words stong enough to revile those he thought of as "the most immoral collection of men I ever knew."After innumerable petitions, "the poor mercantile devils[11]," another of his descriptions, would finally succeed in having their sworn enemy recalled. The hotheaded Scotsman would have to justify his actions before a London court, to be exonerated only after a lengthy trial. Murray, however, would not return to the Quebec where he would be remembered as a friend of the Canadiens.

The governors who succeeded him, the Anglo-Irishman Carleton, in 1776, and the French-speaking Swiss Protestant Haldimand, in 1778, basically followed the same policies in regard to the Canadiens. These three governors more or less considered the Canadiens as children—their children—inexperienced, well-mannered and generally obedient. The governors must be firm but could also show kindness.

There grew up around the governors, starting with Murray, one of the most curious yet revealing phenomena in Quebec and Canadien history: a French Party that would generally defend, as its name indicates, the interests of Canadiens. The thing to remember is that it was comprised essentially of. . . Englishmen. In 1776, there was only one Canadien among the twelve members and, a rarity for the times, he was a Protestant.

The French Party, which would exist until the 1780s, was also called the King's Party. In fact, this was the party of the governor and his friends, whose interests were similar to those of the Canadiens. The Party's often virrulent opposition, the English Party, was led by British merchants.

The French Party did not try very hard to bring over the new English colonists referred to in the Proclamation. In any event, it proved more difficult than expected to attract them to Canada. The Quebec historian J.-P. Wallot informs us that, in the 1780s, Governor Haldimand still dreamed of a pastoral, idyllic Saint Lawrence Valley inhabited solely by Canadiens. Backed by the French Party, the governors also refused to increase the colony's expenses. That would have required new taxes and the convening of an Assembly from which Canadiens would have been excluded.

English-Canadian historians have emphasized the reactionary side of the French Party, which strove to preserve a Canadien society that was no doubt pleasant, yet feudal, fixed in the past and outdated. The British merchants from Montreal who demanded the convening of the Assembly were perhaps less agreeable, but they were not systematically resistant to change. They wanted to develop the country. The survival of the Canadiens went against the flow of history and it wasn't wise to encourage it.

This interpretation, which would be picked up by Lord Durham in his famous report, related Anglo-Saxon values to progress, and it did not take into account a major fact: the action of the French Party was only slightly inspired by humanitarian interests. The competent administrators, Murray and Carleton, were also influenced by *Realpolitik*, an accurate appreciation of England's long-term interests.

Because these Canadiens, even though they had just been conquered, were much stronger than they seemed. They could not be assimilated in this country where they had put down such sturdy roots and where they made up almost the entire population. There was really no choice but to treat them with tact. When the rumble of revolt began to be heard in the southern colonies, it was clear they would have to be won over.

*

As for the seigneurs, the initial attitude of the British military, who had to govern a conquered population, was to hope that as many as possible of these possible troublemakers would emigrate to France. But Murray was an aristocrat. At a time when the American colonists were showing more and more insolence toward the English motherland, he had difficulty resisting his admiration for the order and civility that the seigneurial system maintained in Canadian social relations. It has been said that his ambition was to become a seigneur himself. His successor Carleton, whose wife had grown up at Versailles, would also be tempted to consider the seigneurs as privileged intermediaries. He would even envision having some of them on his Council.

These illusions would not stand the test of reality. The seigneurs were not the leaders of the Canadiens. They never really had been, even under the French regime. The European feudal system transplanted to New France was a watered-down version. After one hundred and fifty years of implantation on a new continent, Canadien society had become profoundly egalitarian, essentially American in this regard.

After the Conquest, the seigneurs did not play a major role. They did not have what today we would call a political base. Some would become personally active[12], often as merchants. Their insistence on keeping seigniorial rights that had become unjustified privileges and their sometimes conspicuous collaboration with the Conqueror, made them unpopular in the eyes of the Habitants. The Canadien seigneurs had not shown themselves unworthy of their compatriots under the French regime, but they were now in that cul de sac which Philippe Aubert de Gaspé described so well in his book, *Les Anciens Canadiens*.

The Church soon became the Conqueror's only go-between, unavoidably so. In a country where there were no municipal institutions, the parish constituted the privileged framework for the Habitants. Unless they wanted to impose a reign of terror, the English administration needed the Church, if only to inform the Canadiens of their instructions.

Catholicism was the hard core of the Canadien identity at a time when the religious domain occupied a considerable portion of the political field. This had been the subject of nine articles in the Capitulation of Montreal in 1760. Canadiens had been granted "free exercise of the Catholic religion in its entirety," yet the French King's nomination of a new bishop had been refused[13].

It is interesting to examine the troubled and sometimes camouflaged relationships woven between Governor Murray and Briand, the future Bishop. Briand established, on the Canadien side, the only real political management system of the Conquest. Even though this system was only partial, Quebecers still experience its consequences. From these dusty chapters of religious history we can learn political lessons that are still valuable.

In the beginning, however, this marriage of reason between the Canadien Church and the English State had everything against it. At that time, England was still virulently anti-Catholic and especially anti-Papist: during his coronation, the King swore to cut down the abhorred Papacy. The Canadien Church was Gallican by tradition, which did not help matters. That meant its first loyalty was not to the Vatican, but to the King of France, the one who named the bishops under the Ancien Regime. London didn't relish choosing between Rome and Paris.

So, as if nothing had happened, London reneged on some of the promises made to the Canadiens at the Capitulation of Montreal. For the first time, the conquered tasted their Conqueror's duplicity. The freedom of religion granted to Canadiens by the Treaty of Paris in 1764 was qualified as follows: "Insofar as British laws allow[14]." The catch was that English laws allowed nothing, or almost. The Canadien Church would have to negotiate everything.

The protagonists were Murray, whom we know, and Briand, who at first glance was not a very likeable character. He had the unhappy role of the collaborator, which he played—to quote a contemporary — with the subtlety of a snake. Neither too proud nor too frank, he was well suited to negotiate with the Conqueror. He knew what he wanted, when to yield and just how far he could go. At times he reminds us of Talleyrand, that other tortuous ecclesiastic who knew how to negotiate. But the timid and astute Briand would not need to give up his cloth or change allegiance twenty times in order to play a leading political role. For thirty years, in Canada, he would be known simply as "the Bishop."

For the time being, he was merely the new head of the Canadien Church. He was more or less chosen by Murray in 1764 because of his poor financial state. In 1762, during the period of idyllic military occupation, the governor had already graced him with a gift of £ 20. The relationship was at first very unequal and to the disadvantage of the conquered. But don't take this man for an illegitimate puppet parachuted into the system by the governor. Mgr. Briand was the Vicar General of Quebec and protégé of the last Bishop of New France, Mgr. de Pontbriand. He had been elected on the second ballot by his peers, after his colleagues had at first preferred Mgr. Montgolfier. But in the eyes of Murray, who vetoed his appointment, Mgr. Montgolfier had the handicap of being rector of the Sulpicians of Montreal and, therefore, financially independent.

With the Royal Proclamation, Murray had received precise instructions from London: the Canadiens would be gradually induced to embrace the Protestant religion, and Rome should not be permitted to exercise power in the colony. So, Briand would have to use politics, play the courtier. Soon after the Proclamation came into effect, he left for London to lobby. He stayed there fourteen months to become familiar with English politics. He had three priorities: maintain discipline within the clergy; preserve Catholic doctrine; and get himself nominated Bishop.

Briand began by telling his priests to be careful. The situation was difficult and they owed allegiance to a government hostile to their religion. They were not to become involved in public affairs, even in the confessional, and they were to respect the law. Priests visiting Quebec could pay a courtesy call on the governor, who would appreciate this. But under no circumstances were they to make suggestions or pass complaints to him. Briand threatened eternal damnation for delinquents. And there would be some: one was Roubaud, an unfrocked Jesuit briefly taken up by Murray, who believed in the possibility of gradually bringing the Canadiens to renounce their religion.

The Habitants would be allowed to practise their Catholic rites, to which they were greatly attached, but on condition that they leave alone the real problem area: "Roman heresy"—in other words, Catholic ideology. The subtle difference between the two terms should not fool us about the importance of what was at stake: the consequences are still with us today. In the middle of the 18th century in the Western World, politics and religion were tightly knit; religious ideology carried substantial political weight. Catholic ideology was imprinted on the fabric of

Canadien society. Briand would not compromise on what was known then as the Dogma.

But, above all, England was dead set against a bishop. In London, Briand was offhandedly told by Lord Shelbourne, the young Minister of the Colonies, that the Canadiens only had to do as the Catholics in Maryland: practise their religion without a bishop. Even the Vatican would be happy with an apostolic vicar. The status of a bishop named by Rome would also be an important source of power, assurance of a minimum of autonomy from the British government; and, through the nomination of new priests, it would be insurance for the future. The status of Bishop was the thing Briand wanted most.

At last, Murray—assured of Briand's reliability and convinced of the rightness of his cause—pleaded for his new friend before a reticent English government. On March 16, 1766, Briand was consecrated Bishop of Canada, or rather, in the words of the pejorative English title of the time, the Superintendent of the Romish Religion—Henry VIII was not quite dead. But to everyone in Canada, from the Governor to the Habitants, Briand would be known as "the Bishop"—much to the dismay of the future Anglican Bishop, who would have difficulty swallowing the affront.

In a highly symbolic coincidence, the new Bishop arrived in Quebec on June 18, 1766, just a few hours after Murray's departure for London, to defend himself against the accusations of the British merchants. Briand found a letter of congratulations from the former Governor, placing the Canadiens in his good care.

It is difficult not to see in this astonishing greeting, which was far more than symbolic, a real transfer of power. If Murray had been only the Conqueror, it would have been ridiculous of him to entrust the Canadiens to the good care of their natural leader. But there was nothing crazy about his letter. By 1766, Murray was more than a Conqueror. In a way, he was a leader of the Canadiens, recognized as such and acting as such.

Despite their friendship, the relationship between Briand and Murray could never have been more than one of the conquered and his conqueror. They were in a situation outside their control. Briand's power in relation to Murray's successor, Carleton, would be more extensive; he was now Bishop. This power was undoubtedly due to his intrinsic strength, and to that of the Canadiens whom he represented. But he had also taken advantage of Murray's help—Murray the Canadien. This process would continue during the rule of the French Party under

Carleton, one of those responsible for the Quebec Act, and then later under Haldimand, although to a lesser degree.

During this crucial period in the development of their collective identity, the Canadiens had, *de facto*, a partially English elite, which often controlled the colony's political power, to the advantage of the conquered. For the Canadiens and their descendants, that was their fortune... and their misfortune.

Eighteen years before the Irish Catholics obtained the right to possess or inherit, the Canadiens already had their own Roman Bishop; Catholic doctrine was intact and the Canadien Church was united. But a price had been paid. The Canadien Church had pledged allegiance in order to obtain the Conqueror's recognition of its power. Later, when Briand had received Rome's permission to choose a successor, on his own volition he submitted his nominee to Carleton for his approval.

The stakes in the negotiations between Murray and Briand were the heart of the Canadien identity of yesterday and the source of Quebec power of today. The authority that Briand was able to maintain over the clergy evolved into the Quebec government's control over the institutions of its specificity: educational establishments; municipal corporations; and the hospital network. The Catholic Dogma of 1760 has become the power in the civil and social fields.

The status of Bishop nominated by Rome was, finally, the beginning of Quebec's particular status as the only province within Canada controlled by Francophones.

*

The Church's political role at that time could only have been partial because the Canadien society was above all a civil society. What this society did not have in order to truly manage the Conquest politically was a bourgeois class, like that developed throughout the rest of the Western World in the 17th and 18th centuries[15]. This bourgeoisie was the dynamic class of the period, politically and economically. It was the conscience of the different budding national identities, and it controlled the newborn power of information. No newspaper was ever published in New France. The first Canadian newspaper was the bilingual *Gazette de Québec*, founded in 1764.

Elsewhere, a similar bourgeoisie was preparing for the War of Independence in the United States and the Great Revolution in France. Without such a politically active class, the young Canadien identity could not collectively become aware of the implications of the abandonment/conquest of 1760-63. The Canadiens could not, therefore, develop concepts or a relevant political strategy to enable them, over time, to rise above the event.

Unable to react, then, except as individuals, the Canadiens didn't recover from the initial shock, which was almost immediately buried deep in the collective subconscious. Briefly, during the depression following the aborted Rebellion of 1837, the Canadiens became aware of the Conquest. Everything indicates that it still exists in the collective subconscious of today's Quebecers and Canadians.

The concept of political integration of an event such as the Conquest is, in itself, neutral. It implies neither acceptance nor rejection of the event in question but simply taking it into consideration. The existence of a bourgeoisie developed after 1763 would, therefore, not necessarily have been an additional guarantee of the Canadiens' survival. They might even have been assimilated more rapidly if their bourgeois class, perhaps for economic reasons, had preferred such an option.

A bourgeoisie that could have survived the Conquest would, more probably, have passed on a more realistic and efficient political strategy to those who would become, in 1791, Lower Canada's first parliamentarians. This perhaps would have enabled the Canadien nation to avoid the disaster of the aborted Rebellion of 1837 and realize its hope of independence.

But, history cannot be rewritten. You try to understand what happened so you are better prepared for the future.

THE CANADIEN NATION

The absence of a well-established bourgeois class in 1760 explains why the Canadiens' nationalism remained weak. In any case, the era of nationalism would not truly begin until the French Revolution, thirty years later.

As individuals, the Habitants experienced the Conquest, as we have seen, without too much difficulty. They suffered the effects of war and then passed into a state of fear. They were reassured during the military occupation and became attached to Murray; having feared for their religion, they would rejoice at having a Bishop. For many years, they would remain mystified by so many uncertainties and changes. Or so it would seem.

But we mustn't confuse weakness with nonexistence. A nationalist embryo was already growing within Canada and would be nourished by the Conquest. The expressions "patrie" and "nous" started to be used in public and private documents. The Habitants could not help but notice that something was happening, something that affected them collectively as Canadiens. This awareness of a common condition and interest was a catalyst for nationalist reflexes. Carleton soon noticed what he called the Canadiens' "group" or "national" spirit. His skill was to exploit this reality, which he could not dissipate.

New France's most intensive period of development coincided with the beginning of Louis XIV's personal reign. Of the ten thousand colonists who crossed the Atlantic during the French Regime, more than three thousand arrived between 1665 and 1672. Canada was the only settlement of a France historically at its peak and exercising an incontestable hegemony over the Western World. There is no doubt that, under the modest surface of Canadien society, there was a lot of energy and concentrated will power.

The events of the past two hundred years are ample proof of the vitality of this collectivity. The sixty-five thousand silent conquered people of 1760 are the ancestors of more than twelve million North Americans of today—more than half of whom still speak French. It would have been dangerous to stage a frontal attack against this formidable latent force.

At first, the Habitants remained silent, passive. The situation of some individuals improved after the French Regime; the fate of a yet-to-be-born nation was not their responsibility. But they were there, essentially spectators of their collective destiny. This inertia, though, was more of a force than appeared at first glance; it had adapted to an almost dead-end situation. Revolt would have been literally suicidal, assimilation unthinkable or, more simply, impossible. It was the French Party that led most of the fight against the Proclamation.

As for the Canadiens, the Church would assure the basic and inevitable collective management needs of the abandonment/conquest. But there were some signs of activity, at least. On October 26, 1764, seven Canadien jurists (Perreault, Bonneau, ...) petitioned the governor to be dissociated from a request presented in their name by English jurists. They wanted to be judged as French, by the French, in accordance with ancient custom and in their maternal language.

This reference to language was rare at the time. Even at the beginning of the repressive regime established by the Royal Proclamation, official documents were automatically in French and English. This satisfied the Canadiens. Their collective identity was based more on French civil rights and the Catholic religion (neither of which was recognized) than on language.

Even as early as 1765, a single passive gesture of resistance would not go unnoticed: the total lack of enthusiasm by the Canadiens for enlisting to put down the rebellion of the former French ally, Chief Pontiac—despite pressing requests from Murray and Mgr. Briand.

Fifteen years after the Conquest, the invasion of Canada in 1775-1776 by American rebels revolting against England would shed light on what the Habitants really thought. They are somewhat the heroes of our history; it is hard not to wonder what their silence hid.

*

In 1774, England adopted the Quebec Act. This Act took into account the consequences of the failure of the Royal Proclamation of 1763: English colonists had not come; Canada remained massively French. With the revolt rumbling in the south, it was essential to win over the British Majesty's "new subjects."

Not surprisingly, many historians consider this the most positive piece of legislation in favour of the Canadiens that has ever emerged from a British government. They obtained recognition of the basic elements of their old national rights: Catholicism and French civil law. The Quebec Act took into account the fact that the Canadiens were not English and never would be, at least not in the foreseeable future. The genius of this Act was in letting the Canadiens be themselves, while remaining British subjects. According to some historians, these were the beginnings of the British Commonwealth.

The Quebec Act also took into account broader geopolitical considerations, in the context of the American War of Independence about to begin. Canada, whose territory had been reduced in 1763 to the inhabited banks of the Saint Lawrence, had regained in part the expansive frontiers of the former New France. The new Province of Quebec took back the territory between the Ohio and the Mississippi. The Americans quickly understood the message: at their expense, England would become heir to the immense empire that France had founded in the New World in the 17th century. To achieve this goal, England bet on the Canadiens, who still made up almost the entire population of this territory.

The Americans were furious. They saw themselves relegated to their narrow coastal strip along the Atlantic. The adoption of the Quebec Act, accelerated by the grumbling of revolt in the southern colonies, would in turn feed the insurrection. Troubles exploded in Lexington and Concord, Massachusetts, in May 1755, just a few days before the new legislation came into effect. The American War of Independence had begun, and the rebels almost immediately attacked British America: Canada was invaded...barely fifteen years after the Conquest. For the first time, the Canadiens had a card to play.

The colony's English merchants quickly revealed themselves pro-American. They hoped to rid themselves of the French Party and obtain—at last—the Assembly that the Quebec Act had refused them yet again. As expected, the Canadien elites—the Church and, even more, the seigneurs—took the side of the British. Briand was still there, threatening to deprive the Canadiens of the sacraments if they refused to enlist or if they helped the Americans.

This time, the Habitants really showed their colours. They did not appreciate the over-zealous manner of either their priests or their seigneurs. One parishioner even dared to heckle his priest during a sermon: "That's enough preaching for the English[16]." The Canadiens would lean toward the rebel American side, helping when the time was right or when they seemed likely to win. That would happen often during this war of successive offensives and retreats. In the temporarily occupied southern part of the province, the Americans even succeeded in establishing two Canadien regiments.

Such a commitment was the exception. The Habitants were repelled at the thought of becoming involved in what they considered English squabbling. They were wary, for memories of the French regime were still fresh in their minds. The Canadiens could not have complete faith in the words of their sworn enemy, those Bostonians who only yesterday had been fanatically anti-Papist. Their contradictory language would not go unnoticed. They claimed to be friends of the Canadiens, but they did not have words strong enough to reproach London with its recognition of Catholicism in the Quebec Act. It was the last straw when the Canadiens' supposed liberators tried to pay for their purchases with paper money. That brought back too directly the bad memories of the end of the French Regime.

All things considered, then, the Canadiens were neutral. This new version of their power of inertia would enable England to win its bet. There is no doubt that the English would not have been able to keep Canada if the Canadiens had come in fully on the side of the Americans.

On December 31, 1775, the combined forces of Generals Montgomery and Arnold would fail in the attempt to take Quebec. The following spring, Benjamin Franklin, the man whose eloquence had seduced Versailles and convinced France to offer its military support to the new Republic, would leave empty-handed from still-occupied Montreal.

By refusing to clearly take sides, despite favours from the Conqueror, promises from the Americans, and exhortations from the Bishop, the Canadiens demonstrated their existence as a political force for the first time since the Conquest. No one was pleased: the Americans would leave without having freed this worthless and backward collectivity; the old Canadien elites had met their match.

Carleton would never again see them in the same light, these people he thought he knew so well. "There is nothing to fear from them, while we are in a state of prosperity, and nothing to hope for, while in distress[17]," he would comment later, disenchanted. He who had promised Lord Shelbourne in 1767 that the country would always be inhabited by Canadiens, he who had been one of those principally responsible for the Quebec Act, had changed. The charm was gone. Already, during the War of 1774-1776, the governor had sometimes seemed more concerned with the American prisoners than with the Canadiens. To him, the former became potential English colonists, the latter were deceiving opportunists.

Carleton left Canada shortly afterward, in 1778. When he returned as Governor for the second time, in 1786, he came as Lord Dorchester, no longer the same man. Carleton had been the worthy successor of Murray as protector of the Canadiens. Lord Dorchester would devote most of his time to the American loyalists who had recently come to live in Canada. (He used to be honoured with the title "Father of English Canada" in English Canadian history books.) This was the beginning of what would later be known as the Canadian duality.

In fact, the American Revolution created English Canada. Americans who wanted to remain loyal to the British Crown began moving in to this part of the continent still controlled by the English. These "Loyalists" were another vanquished people, but one able to refuse a conquest. Between 1780 and 1784, the population of British origin tripled, growing from fifteen thousand to forty-five thousand. Some Loyalists installed themselves in the Gaspé Region and the Eastern Townships, but the majority went to the Maritimes, leading to the creation of New Brunswick. They also laid the foundation of what would become, in 1791, Upper Canada.

The Canadiens' neutrality had kept the northern part of the continent in the hands of England. But English tutelage had allowed the Canadiens to escape what had seemed to be their unavoidable destiny: annexation to the neighbouring American republic—twenty-five times larger in population and convinced that its "manifest destiny" was to take possession of the entire North American continent. Beginning their inescapable ascent to world hegemony, the United States would form a "true nation." They did not need the particularities of the Old World. They quickly assimilated the 100,000 Germans who were living in Pennsylvania during the War of Independence and they "folklorized" Louisiana, yielded to them by Napoleonic France in 1803.

At the side of the young Yankee giant, Canada would be born— already old and looking towards the past—of the improbable marriage between the Canadiens of the Sun King and the Americans who wanted to remain under the King of England. The leftovers of two empires!

*

It was a Frenchman by the name of Mesplet who printed the American propaganda inviting Canadiens to join in the revolt against England. He did not return with the American invaders and settled down in Canada. In 1778 he founded *La Gazette littéraire de Montréal,* the first French paper in the colony. The Canadian press was born.

The Canadiens were not insensitive to the ideas of freedom left in the wake of the Americans. In 1784, they denounced the nondemocratic character of the Governor's Council: the paternalism of a French Party which had already run its course no longer sufficed. As a result, in 1791, England granted them a House of Assembly, one of the first in the world. The sons of the Habitants of 1760 would become parliamentary representatives of Lower Canada. For the colony was now divided in two: the Lower Canada of the Canadiens, and the Upper Canada of the Loyalists, the Quebec and Ontario of today.

While the waves of revolution of the great French nation were breaking on Europe, its little Canadian cousin was taking flight. A wind of freedom was blowing everywhere in this beginning of the nineteenth century. The new *Nation canadienne* was looking toward freedom within the Empire, under the indispensable protection of the English motherland against the too-obvious objectives of the Americans. For a long time, the charismatic leader of the nation, Louis-Joseph Papineau, thought that Canada would see happy days only under the aegis of

England. In 1820, when George III was dying, he praised the British Monarch highly, comparing him favourably to Louis XV, the Canadiens' last French King.

The Americans invaded Canada again, in 1812. This time, the Canadiens did take up arms, often fervently; Salaberry drove back the invaders at Chateauguay with troops almost entirely Canadien. The Canadiens were defending their land, Canada, in which they would be the majority of the population until the 1830s.

The new Canadien parliamentarians were lawyers, doctors, journalists, and small businessmen. They entered politics en masse, under the flag of nationalism, and unearthed some of Murray's and Carleton's ideas. The *Parti canadien* distrusted the public spending programs, which the Assembly did not control and which favoured the English of Lower Canada. The French Party was dead. The *Chateau Clique*, the English Party, now reigned, to the detriment of the interests of the Canadien majority.

The representatives of the *Parti canadien* believed in the virtues of the British parliamentary system. They adhered to English democratic values. Like the Reformist Party of neighbouring Upper Canada, the Canadiens asked that the Assembly have real control over government spending. The Governor refused; the Canadien representatives refused to vote the credits; the Governor dissolved the Assembly; the population re-elected the same representatives. And round we go again ... featuring the fiery speeches of Papineau, the insults of English papers, and petitions to London. Around again, one notch higher. Around and around...

In 1831, unknown to anyone, the anchor was tripped. The English Minister for the Colonies, Lord Goderich, proposed a compromise: the Assembly could control expenses as long as it approved en bloc the salaries for members of the Executive Council. That was the original proposal put forward by the moderates of the *Parti Canadien*. But, in 1826, that party became the radical *Parti Patriote*. They demanded, now, that members of the Executive Council be elected and that the *Chateau Clique* disappear. They wanted the House of Assembly to govern. On the recommendation of Papineau, the Assembly rejected Lord Goderich's proposal. England would go no further.

Although the moderates were falling away and the Church was flatly opposed, Papineau remained confident. The Canadiens' cause was just; revolt was flaring in Upper Canada for similar reasons. The *London Times* even wrote that it was not worth staying in Canada if one had to stay there by force.   In any event, it was soon too late: English troops fired on a crowd in Montreal, killing two Canadiens. Through Papineau, the outraged Canadien people voiced their national pride and, shortly, their wish for independence.

The rest, like the Plains of Abraham, is well known: the 1837-1838 insurrection in the two Canadas. The rebellion would be harshly repressed by British power. Eighteen patriots would be hanged, fifty-eight deported. Many others would be imprisoned, some of whom would later play an important political role, especially Louis-Hippolyte LaFontaine and Georges-Etienne Cartier.

Unfortunately, no elite had bequeathed to the Canadien parliamentarians, those sons and brothers of the Habitants, a political philosophy that took into account the experience of the Conquest. Of course there was the Church, but the Church... So politics went on as if the Conquest had never taken place. The *Parti Canadien* behaved as if Lower Canada were merely another English colony that wanted to be autonomous. In the end, the *Parti Patriote* wanted independence without having organized the uprising and without having the means to do so. They had forgotten that England was not just a motherland in need of coaxing: she was also the Conqueror of the Canadiens.

They had also forgotten that, for the first time, there were as many English in Canada as there were Canadiens. Lord Durham would pass down the verdict in the name of the Conqueror. The Upper and Lower Canadas would be united; the Canadiens, soon to be a minority, would be assimilated, and this would lead to the now inevitable self-government of the colony. The Upper Canadian reformists would gradually get what they had been fighting for.

The *Nation canadienne* would never recover. From now on, its people would be known as French Canadians.

CHAPTER 2

A Country Built on the Conquest

September 22, 1988. The *Toronto Star*, this daily which is said to be the effective vehicle for the fears of English-Canadian nationalists about Free Trade. Page 8, a large picture of a smiling Jean Chrétien. The former Liberal minister welcomes in Toronto four hundred supporters: "John Chretien welcomes some of the. . . "

John Chretien?

Jean Chrétien is well-liked in English Canada, where everyone knows that the "little guy from Shawinigan" is a Francophone from Quebec. For the past few years he has been practising his profession of lawyer in the Ontario capital; there has never been any question of the Canadian loyalty of this Quebecer who convinced his compatriots to vote "Non" in the 1980 Referendum.

That is all it took for the *Toronto Star* to christen "John Chretien," the man who was aspiring to become Canada's next Prime Minister.

THE QUEBECOIS HEART

Look at a Canadian history book used in English high schools during the 1930s [1]. That was thirty years before modern Quebec nationalism, before the actions of French Power in Ottawa greatly changed the image that English Canadians had of Quebec and Canada. In the Dominion of Canada of Prime Minister Richard Bennett, when the Catholic province of Quebec was still "priest-ridden," to quote a cliché of the times, you would expect to read a history of Canada that was rather different from what was still being taught, yesterday, in Quebec schools.

Emphasis there was placed on the happy period of New France, then we moved quickly to contemporary Quebec and Canada. We didn't spend much time on the emotionally draining hundred years between 1763 and 1867, the genesis of modern Canada. By comparison, what English-Canadian college students learned in 1934 about the history of the country should help to understand further the foundation of the anglophone side of the Canadian identity of today.

First, a surprise, and a big one. The traditional English version of the history of Canada differs from the French version, but not where one would expect. For New France is there, in detail, spread over several chapters: Champlain, Frontenac, the Habitants and the seigneurs, and the Deportation of the Acadians. Almost everything that was being taught in Quebec is included. Except the emotion, of course. And there are not many distortions, either, considering the period.

As expected, the basic difference is the emphasis placed on the 1780s foundation of what would become English Canada. More importance is placed, too, on the pre-Confederation period. As for the Loyalists (those Americans who paid the price of remaining faithful to the King of England), passages of lyricism resemble old French-Canadian histories that tell the story of the blessed era of New France's pioneers.

But how is it that English Canadians of 1934 learned so much about New France? It was such a long time before bilingualism became fashionable with their elites—a time when they more-or-less openly would label Quebec as backward? The key to the enigma is in one little sentence, at first glance harmless, that concludes the episode of the American invasion of Canada in 1812: "Once again, the American invaders were repelled, as in 1776, as in 1690."

No problem with 1776. The newly-British Canada had been invaded for the first time by the Americans during their War of Independence against England. But 1690? That is one of the most celebrated episodes in the history of New France. The prickly Governor Frontenac took a Louis-the-Fourteenth tone in hurling at Phipps' envoy—sent to demand his surrender—a tirade that every little Quebecer used to know by heart: "Go tell your master that I will answer by the mouth of my cannon." How can the British Canada that drove back the Americans in 1812 be linked to the New France that stood up to the English in 1690?

There is obviously only one explanation, which says a great deal about Canada: not only was the country built on New France (an objective reality) but it very early wanted to inherit and continue the American empire that France had founded in the seventeenth century. And to do this—a point of first importance—in the face of the Americans. In fact, on investigation, Frontenac's enemy, Phipps, was an Englishman from the colony of Massachusetts...one of those "Bostonians" who would later become the Americans.

The Canadian identity has very well integrated this reality, which English-Canadian school children were taught from 1934: England took over from France in the north of the continent, against its old American colonies. The history of New France is an integral part of Canadian history. It is not a mere coincidence that the country has always called itself Canada, under the English regime as it was under the French.

A contemporary demonstration of this phenomenon is the in-depth knowledge that many English-Canadian intellectuals and academics have of Quebec. It is possible to read refined analyses of almost every facet of Quebec society, written by English Canadians who sometimes give the impression of knowing more about Quebec than Quebecers themselves. A part of the English-Canadian elite seems literally fascinated by the Quebec identity and its deeply rooted nature.

Quebec is also, we mustn't forget, in the physical heart of Canada. This territorial aspect has always been an essential component of the official Canadian identity. The country's motto is *A Mari Usque ad Mare*: from one ocean to the other. It is emotionally vital to Canadian identity that the country spread across the map from the Atlantic to the Pacific, all in one sweep, all in one colour.

The fact that Canada was built on Quebec and that it cannot imagine existing without it was put aside, if not forgotten, by the Quebec nationalism of the 1960s—for reasons easy to understand. Given that England had tried to make the Anciens Canadiens disappear in 1763 and 1840, given that their descendants have suffered more than their share of exploitation and humiliation at the hands of the English, and given that the Quebecers of today have great difficulty in getting themselves recognized as a modest distinct society, it is no wonder they are a little bit sceptical when they are told that Canada wanted to continue New France, and that the Franco-Canadian identity is at the heart of the Canadian identity of today. This is, nevertheless, a historic reality that is difficult to deny.

The reverse is not true, however. If it is very difficult for Canada to imagine itself without Quebec, that province has always had the possibility—and at times the need—to imagine existing outside of Canada. The intellectual elites and the creators, who are at the heart of Quebec nationalism, have traditionally taken no interest in English Canada. Even in a field like political science, where the specific nature of English-Canadian culture is incontestable and frequently related to the Quebec reality, priority is often given to Europe and the United States. In French Quebec, there is a taste for things international and American that is in part a flight from Canada.

THE EFFECT OF THE CONQUEST

Informed English Canadians generally admit that Canada was built starting with Quebec. George Grant, in his classic *Lament for a Nation*, opportunely reminded us of this in the 60s, before the reforms of the Trudeau era brought a new and striking demonstration of this reality. The reality, besides, is an integral part of the official Canadian ideology. In 1982, the former Governor-General of Canada, Jules Léger, described himself as the sixty-third Governor of the country since Champlain. That is not the problem. It is, rather, that Mr. Léger added "in an unbroken historical lineage[2].

From 1608 to 1982 without a break...Canada recognizes New

France, the contribution of a Quebec that it would not know how to do without. But there is silence on, and denial of, the tremendous rupture of the battle on the Plains of Abraham, which decided that America would be Anglophone. The system does not take into account the permanent political effects of the Conquest. Well, modern Canada was built not only on the Anciens Canadiens of 1760, but on Canadiens who had been conquered.

This refusal to recognize that there was a break in the lineage always makes you a little sad when it comes from a Francophone, even if that is bound to happen more and more often as time passes. It is the sign of a separation, and profound alienation, in regard to the identity of the Anciens Canadiens. But this attitude is, at first sight, more easily understood in an Anglophone. After all, it is not really his problem. It was the ancestors of Quebecers who lived through the Conquest, and it is their descendants who still suffer some of the effects, real or imagined.

There is no great collective trauma passed to the descendants of the Conquerors, on the other hand. In all honesty, many would admit that they take a certain satisfaction from it. Unless you are a masochist, it is the situation that offers the most advantages…especially if you know what it is like to be on the other side. That was the case, don't forget, of the first English Canadians, the Loyalists, who had just suffered a bitter defeat at the hands of the Americans.

We must remember, too, that a large number of English Canadians are no longer of Anglo-Saxon descent. It is not surprising that studies have hardly ever been done on the effects of the Conquest on English Canada or on the modern Canadian identity. On the brink of the year 2000, it seems outdated, even a little ridiculous, to continue to dwell on this antiquated event that has already been sifted over and over. Most Canadians have never heard of it. Those who do know about it would think that it's the same old song of the Quebecers—who complain, like spoiled kids who will always complain, whatever concessions are made. And God knows they have been made…!

Such an attitude is explicable, even understandable. But that does not make it any less regrettable, because the 1760 Conquest had a basic effect on the collective identity of all today's Canadians: from the Torontonian of Italian origin, through all the ordinary Canadians and Quebecers who make up the country, to the American retiree in Victoria. Not being aware of the fact does not change the reality.

The roots of this influence go back to the beginnings of the country. English Canada has never existed alone, without its French counterpart. The Quebec identity, if it is able, because of its autonomous origins, to see itself outside Canada, has nonetheless benefitted from an English input at an important time in its historic genesis. The two identities have been related for more than two hundred years. They have penetrated each other, are present in each other's core. The Conquest could not have affected one without affecting the other. You might even believe that, in the past thirty years, it has become just as much a Canadian problem as a Quebec one. Paradoxically, Canadians would have to confront the problem, even if Quebec had to leave.

It is important to note that the problem is not simply that the Canadian identity and the Quebec identity are related. Faced with the tremendous rising of American strength in the Northern continent, the Anciens Canadiens and the Loyalists needed each other in order to survive the birth of the United States. Even if the Anciens Canadiens had not been conquered, it probably would have been in their best interests to join the American Loyalists. In itself, the union between the two groups benefitted both sides. It is where you must look for the origins of what is politically functional in Canada and of what has enabled it to exist as a country for two hundred years.

The problem is that the relationship between the Anciens Canadiens and the Loyalists was established on the basis of the Conquest, which nourished the Canadian identity and on which the Canada of today is still built. The process has accentuated over these past years. Now it threatens the healthy aspects of the relationship between the Canadian identity and the Quebec identity. At worst, it is the integrity of the Quebec society and the integrity of Canada that are at stake.

The basic dynamic is relatively simple. For almost its entire, lengthy gestation (eighty years, from the 1760 Conquest to the 1840 Union), Canada was made up of a francophone majority under British control. The English-Canadian population of American origin increased only gradually, to become a majority in the 1830s. That situation could only have deeply affected the nature of the developing country.

Habits were borrowed from both sides. And then there was the essential political consequence of any conquest: the conqueror's profitable confiscation of part of the power that stems naturally from the collective identity of the conquered. By definition, collective identities are generators of a political power that represents their will to live.

At the end of the 1770s, the American Revolution gave birth to English Canada; those inhabitants of the Thirteen Colonies who were against the American Revolution emigrated to the north, where they found the Anciens Canadians solidly rooted and under British control. It is important to remember that these Loyalists were not English people from England, like Murray and Carleton. They were Americans.

They quickly took advantage of the political effects of the Conquest, of the strength of the Anciens Canadiens, which, at that time, was one of inertia. The Canadiens' neutrality under British domination prevented the Americans from conquering the country. This helping hand, as involuntary as it was decisive, enabled English Canada to be born and the first English Canadians to settle. Governor Carleton's role in this process would be important; at first a friend of the Anciens Canadiens, he later became the father of English Canada under the name Lord Dorchester.

The Loyalists would soon be joined by other American immigrants, non-Loyalists this time. Politically neutral, they emigrated to Canada for economic reasons, in search of the "New Frontier": Upper Canada, the Ontario of today. During the second American invasion of Canada in 1812, these non-Loyalist Americans made up the majority of Canada's English population. So, the English Canadians profited a second time by the political effects of the existence of the Anciens Canadiens. In their defence of Canada, these Anciens Canadiens showed a fervour that contrasted with the lack of enthusiasm sometimes shown by an anglophone population that was mostly American and non-Loyalist.

In the years to follow, from 1815 to 1850, Canada would receive a large number of immigrants from the British Isles—more than a million. But it is vital for our thesis to remember that while the English-Canadian identity was being formed, during the gestation of modern Canada, the country was populated by a conquered Ancien Canadien majority, by a small number of British administrators and servicemen, and by Americans, most of them non-Loyalist.

In the beginning, English-Canadian society was too similar to American to justify the creation of an independent state, even if the political desire had been there. The United States was too powerful, the first English Canadians too few, and too American. Fortunately for them, they found in Canada the Anciens Canadiens, whose collective identity had been well-defined since the beginning of the eighteenth century. People they could count on. Because these Anciens Canadiens were conquered, the Loyalists, with the support of the British administration, could use the Canadien identity politically in the new country they wished to build.

The availability, because of the Conquest, of the solid collective identity of the first Canadiens and their descendants, eventually had a perverse effect on English Canada. It made it unnecessary to root its own identity in relation to the American identity, which normally would have been necessary in order to maintain a state separate from the United States in the northern part of the continent. It didn't have to count on certain original characteristics of English Canada, such as the regionalism that was deeply ingrained at first and that gradually degenerated into a much less fertile provincialism.

The English Canadians could choose the easy route. Already very American, they could abandon themselves individually to the delectable temptation of becoming even more so, without having to suffer collectively the political consequences. Quebec was there at the important times, British and available, sending its Cartiers, its Lauriers, its Trudeaus.

From this point of view, the history of Canada can be seen as the Canadian identity's slow yet systematic siphoning of the Quebec identity. The country was obviously more than that. Individually, the Francophones benefitted from belonging to the Canadian federation; collectively, everything indicates that they would have been more quickly assimilated outside Canada. But it is not by chance that the majority of today's descendants of the Canadiens of 1760 who still speak French identify themselves first as Québécois, while the descendants of the American Loyalists of 1780 all became Canadian[4]. There was definitely a transfer of something, somewhere along the line.

In the northern part of the continent, English Canadians founded a state separated from the United States. They gave it its own economic base, and, with the help of Quebec, they developed a political culture whose originality is undeniable. But the English-Canadian society has remained an American society; English-Canadian culture is, in large part, an American culture. English Canada's specificity has always, and above all, been expressed in two fields: political and economic.

This explains the fears of English-Canadian nationalists faced with a liberalization of trade with the United States. Free Trade threatens one of their two domains. Otherwise, in the degree to which the cultural specificity of English Canada diminishes, the Canadian identity tends to concentrate more and more on its political domain. And it is more and more dependent on the confiscation of certain political consequences that stem naturally from Quebec's specificity.

This reality was well-illustrated during the Meech Lake Accord debate. While some English Canadians agreed to recognize Quebec as a distinct society, this was only on the implicit condition that such a recognition not carry with it political power. Obviously, even these Canadians who believed themselves open to the Quebec Fact still adopted, consciously or not, an attitude of conquerors towards it.

CHAPTER 3
French Canada
(1840-1960)

A child is born attached, in all senses of the word, to his mother. Then comes the time when he must lean on his father to break away from his mother and move on to autonomy. That is the ideal.

In reality, the child does not always find the father he needs. He is somewhat dependent on his mother; he has difficulty becoming autonomous. He is ashamed...

In some cultures, the negative aspects of this shame are compensated by mechanisms designed to "save face."

It was not until the Act of Union had clearly identified the consequences of the Patriots' aborted rebellion that the Canadiens, in the process of becoming a minority in their own country and officially dedicated to assimilation, were confronted for the first time with "the unthinkable." We are now at the beginning of the 1840s; eighty years earlier, only the Church had realized the implications of the Conquest.

The shock was terrible. The Canadien elites, on the eve of becoming French Canadians, sank into a brief but intense period of collective depression. Today, to read the protest of journalist Etienne Parent is still moving. To him, the death of the Canadien Nation and the assimilation of his compatriots seemed inevitable.

But Parent soon emerged from his depression, as did other imprisoned Patriots deeply marked by the 1837 defeat: Louis-Hippolyte LaFontaine and Georges-Etienne Cartier. Necessity ruled: they would work under the new regime in defence of French-Canadian rights. Their forced collaboration with the Upper Canadian English would soon produce results they had not even hoped for.

With the aid of Robert Baldwin's Reformists, LaFontaine would gain recognition once more for the French language in United Canada's parliament. Together, in the early 1850s, they would obtain responsible government. In the meantime, the new leader of the French Canadians would endure without flinching the bitter reproaches of his former chief, Papineau. A living myth returned from his American exile, the old Canadian leader now preached in the House the doctrine of annexation to the United States.

It soon became clear that the Union of the two Canadas would be very difficult to administer. To counter a new rise of American imperialism, and at the strong suggestion of England, consideration was given to joining United Canada to the other British colonies in the north of the continent. Because of this, Georges-Etienne Cartier insisted that a federal system be adopted and that French Canadians be given their own government, the one they had sought since the Conquest.

In the process, some of these pragmatic politicians would acquire a taste for things English. Cartier, the principal French-Canadian Father of Confederation, had been accused of treason by the British in 1838, for having fought on the side of the Patriots. He would die as Sir George (without an "s") in London in 1873, anglicized in manner and notably beholden to the new regime.

When the descendants of the Anciens Canadiens obtained their own government in 1867, it marked their first political victory since the Conquest, a victory even more significant because it was not only a concession by the English but a result of the efforts of some of their own people. The misfortune was that this government came a little late. By that time, the French Canadians had become incapable of using fully their new political powers, even though these powers were much more limited than those of today's Quebec government.

In fact, the French Canadians of 1867 were already quite different from their Canadien fathers of 1830. "Patriot" nationalism had at times been unrealistic, but it had always been steadfastly political, based on the takeover of control of Lower Canada's government. After the rebellion's failure, the French-Canadian elites sank gradually into a religious messianism— conservative and anti-state. It was at this time, and not, as is often believed, during the French regime or the Conquest, that the French-Canadian "Church Triumphant", which would play a major political role until 1960, was born. In 1840, the credibility of the Church was at its zenith. The other elites had failed miserably. Only the Church could say: "I told you so."

Couldn't French Canadians attain political self-determination? Were they excluded from economic power, condemned to become a minority? What if that were true: it wasn't a problem, because the mission of the French-Canadian nation was something quite different. At the heart of a materialistic, Protestant continent, it would carry high the torch of spiritual and intellectual values associated with Catholicism. To save the honour of the collectivity, an entire ideology of French Canada's spiritual mission would gradually be established across the country, throughout the continent, and around the world. The politicians of the time, the Cartiers, Lauriers, and Merciers, would have to come to terms with this ideology, which would dominate French Canada from 1860 onward.

Historians have shown that, in the latter half of the deeply imperialistic nineteenth century, the French Canadians were imperialists in their own way, transferring their nationalist energy from the political to the religious sector. It was at this time that Quebec began sending nuns, priests, and bishops everywhere... to the land of the Red River, to Oregon, to Brazil, and even to the Russia of the Czars. One of the greatest moments of French-Canadian nationalism was the 1870 dispatch of a contingent of Zouaves to defend His Holiness, besieged by the new Italy that wanted Rome as its capital.

This flight into religion enabled the French-Canadian identity to "save face" and maintain its psychological integrity, despite the dramatic defeat of 1837-1840. It appeased the painful contact with the repressed collective trauma of the 1763 Conquest. In the Quebec and Canadian reality, the price paid was, nevertheless, considerable. After 1867, it prevented French Canadians from fully using the powers of the first government they had controlled.

A chosen nation is not concerned with provincial administration. While a high-sounding and powerless French-Canadian nationalism attempted to evangelize the universe, and its energies were devoted to defending conservative values inexorably in regression, it proved incapable of taking advantage of some of the opportunities offered by Canadian Confederation.

THE WEST WILL BE ENGLISH

As early as 1774, England had given back to the constricted 1764 Province of Quebec an ample portion of what used to be New France. Montreal regained the back-country it urgently needed to keep control of the fur trade, which had to seek its skins further and further away in the West. A large part of the French regime's economic structure was thus restored.

But, because of the basic effects of the Conquest on psychological, economical, and political levels, it was the newly born English Canada that would profit from this change. English-Canadian historians have brought out this role of Montreal as the support base for the conquest of the West, and of the construction of a larger

Canada from which the Francophones would be excluded, little by little.

Those who continued the fur trade in the West were still mostly French-speaking during the first part of the nineteenth century, a long time after control of this trade had passed into the hands of the English of Montreal. The first language spoken at Fort Edmonton was French. Those who continued the *coureurs de bois* tradition often married natives of the territory, thus laying the foundation of a new, French-majority nation. Manitoba was created in 1870 for this small Métis nation. Originally, it was completely bicultural in fact and in law, endowed with a constitution that copied Quebec's.

The famous Riel affair and then Manitoba's French schools episode marked the failure, by the end of the nineteenth century, of an attempt to establish the French Fact within the new Canada developing in the West. The English group made it very clear that they still considered themselves descendants of the conquerors. They emotionally refused Canadian duality outside Quebec, showing themselves inflexible as regards the fundamentally English nature of this new Canada.

The conservative religious ideology of French Canada, and the spiritual mission it had given itself since the death of the Canadien nation, did the rest. In the ten years from 1870 to 1880, French Canada showed itself to be be incapable of taking over part of this formally bilingual West. Afterward, it was too late. And yet, the Frenco-American population of New England doubled during the same period, from 103,000 in 1870 to 208,000 in 1880.

The federal government was justly reproached for having subsidized the mass arrival of central Europeans to populate the West, while little was being done to prevent the French Canadians from exiling themselves to the United States. But that does not really explain why the West is anglophone today. When the overseas immigrants arrived in this region of the country around 1900, the thrust of the French-Canadian exodus to the United States was already over. And the irremediably English character of the West had been decided much earlier, between 1870 and 1880, by an immigration of people mostly from Ontario.

Of course the Anglo-Saxons of the era—sometimes fanatics, always conquerors—would not offer the Francophones anything. But the French-Canadian mentality of that time also explains the preference for the friendly "Little Canadas," just on the other side of the Quebec border, over the opportunities of the faraway Great Plains, beyond inhospitable Ontario. The disastrous consequences of the ideology developed by French-Canadian nationalism after 1840 in order to save face should be remembered because of the dangers of repeating this process, in the shadow of the 1980 Referendum failure.

In retrospect, the failure to establish Canadian duality in the West was inevitable because of the aftermath of the Conquest, which the episode brought to the surface in both groups. This doomed Canada to become an English country in which French Quebec would become more and more marginal: the bilingual schools issue in Manitoba paved the way to the nationalism centred in Quebec that has been expressed since 1960.

It was not surprising that the Canadian guarantor of this Quebec Nationalism, French Power, based its action on the idea of formal bilingualism of the federation, particularly in the West. That stirred up poignant memories for Canadian Francophones. The zealots of bilingualism tried to convince Quebecers that the country was realizing Henri Bourassa's old dream of a binational Canada. In the West, become totally anglophone, the cosmetics were too superficial to cover the fact that that battle had really been lost more than a century before.

The tragic adventure of the chief of the Métis nation, Louis Riel, hanged to calm the clamour of Ontario Orangemen, stirred up the French Canada of the 1880s. Not well-known by Quebecers today, Riel has become a hero in English Canada and, to some, a Canadian hero *par excellence*. His mystic destiny of the loser fascinates writers such as Margaret Atwood: it causes vague feelings of guilt to surface.

Paradoxically, it was Wilfrid Laurier, the first French Canadian to become Prime Minister of Canada, who would have to sanction the end of separate French schools in Manitoba in 1896. He later presided over the creation of Alberta and Saskatchewan and the enthusiastic launching of the country's new English region: "The twentieth century will belong to Canada!"

The same Laurier, become Sir Wilfrid, would succeed in channelling towards Canada a little of the fervour that the English majority still felt for the British Empire. In this period was born the Canadian national feeling as we generally understand it today. For the first time, English Canadians started to feel occasionally not just British but *Canadian*.

Is it really a coincidence that this sentiment emerged after the first major weakening of Canadian duality, under a French-Canadian Prime Minister? As if, in order for there to be more Canada, there had to be less Quebec.

CANADIAN FEDERALISM

In 1867, the country had just endowed itself with a federal constitution. Georges-Etienne Cartier had pleaded that only such a system would be acceptable to his French-Canadian compatriots; they wanted government for themselves and by themselves, a government that would be sovereign in areas important to them, such as civil law and education. It is well known that the man who was to become the first Canadian Prime Minister, John A. Macdonald, would have preferred a unitary State.

As one would expect, the original text of the Canadian Constitution, the fruits of a compromise between opposing views, had hardly been federal. The 1867 British North America Act centralized all the important powers of the time in Ottawa: it gave the federal government the right to control the provincial governments. That was contrary to one of the principles of federalism, which sees each level of government as sovereign in its area of competency.

At the beginning of the nineteenth century, the takeoff of the West increased English-Canadian regionalism. As well, with the Riel Rebellion, French nationalism became very difficult to manage at the federal level. In order to survive, the regime had to evolve into a decentralized federation—which Canada finally became on the eve of the 1930s Depression.

It is interesting to note that this decentralization was encouraged by the judgments of the highest British court of the time, where Canada's constitutional cases were presented as a last resort. Once again, it was an English power—this time the ceremonial Judicial Committee of His Majesty's Privy Council, in London—that increased the power controlled by the descendants of the Anciens Canadiens.

This period ended with the 1929 Crash. Almost bankrupt, the provinces found themselves incapable of reconstructing the devastated economy of the 1930s. Later, when the "Welfare State" was being built in the euphoria of postwar prosperity, the dynamism of English Canada and the activism of the federal government contrasted strongly with the inertia of a clearly outdated French-Canadian society. With the tacit approval of an increasingly homogeneous English Canada, a profound process of centralization was set in motion . . . and a Quebec huddled over its past could not affect it much.

At the end of the 1950s, Canada was casually changing into a quasi-unitary state. During the glorious age of shared programs, the provinces' role seemed inevitably to deliver the programs decided and planned in Ottawa, under the competent tutelage of anonymous and all-powerful federal mandarins. The Canadian Eisenhower, Louis Stephen Saint-Laurent, presided in an easygoing manner over what was called "cooperative federalism."

The new Ottawa powers were exercised in jurisdictions that were traditionally provincial, as in the case of the famous federal subsidies to universities. At that time, Quebec Premier Maurice Duplessis threatened Quebec educational institutions with severe reprisals if they dared eat from the hand of Ottawa. In the light of English Canada's too-evident desire to appropriate its spoils, the sly politician from Trois-Rivières did what he had to do to maintain control of his troops, like Briand two hundred years earlier.

While Duplessis held the fort, signs of profound change started to manifest themselves in Quebec. The old French-Canadian caterpillar was ending its metamorphosis into a lively Quebec butterfly. At the beginning of the 1960s, the thundercrash of a nationalism centred on Quebec was heard.

CHAPTER 4

Franco-Canadian Nationalism (1960 - 1982)

That was yesterday. And yet, in many ways, it is already long ago, like a dream, something in brackets...It was like the unfortunate *Nation des Patriotes*, which modern Quebec nationalism would unknowingly come to resemble in so many ways.

Unknowingly...or, at least, unwillingly! For Quebec nationalism soon prided itself on being basically new. With the joyous arrogance of youth, it resolutely turned its back on the old French-Canadian nationalism, which was really a reminder of too many defeats and humiliations...of too much shame. In 1962, when the Jean Lesage and Réne Lévesque "equipe de tonnerre" convinced Quebecers that they had to nationalize electrical power in order to become "master in our own house," Duplessis' death only three years earlier already seemed so far away!

Latin-like in this regard, Quebec benignly foreshadowed what would later occur in Spain, Portugal, and Greece: the great release, without shock, after an endless stagnation. The accelerated modernization of a society. If it had not been the Liberal Lesage, it would have been the Unionist Sauvé or someone else who would have presided over this Quiet Revolution. But it had to happen; it had been too long awaited.

We can't say often enough just how much—in the spirit of a generous and prosperous period—Quebec nationalism carried within it something beautiful. It was fundamentally positive and open. This is one reason why it is difficult for many Quebecers of today to accept the death of some of their dreams. These would almost never resemble the crude ethnocentric caricature often drawn of them in the Anglo-Saxon world.

Quebec nationalism soon had its Canada-wide echo under the name French Power. The use of the expression Quebec Nationalism to describe what had happened in Quebec between 1960 and 1982 is really only appropriate for the first years of that period.

Besides, it is deceiving; for this phenomenon was basically two-fold. It is impossible to understand its dynamic if you look at only one of its sides. To describe in their entirety the expressions of Quebec nationalist energy, beginning in the early 1960s, we will use in this book the expression "Franco-Canadian nationalism."

The political action of Quebecers within the federal government affected the entire country, including Quebec. Quebec nationalism, centred on the French province, was without a doubt the major component, and the most flamboyant. But it was the Canadian component, the initially more-or-less marginal French Power, that would finally win the highest stakes.

As early as 1962, an unknown Quebec intellectual, Pierre Elliot Trudeau, had shared with Rene Lévesque his doubts about the possibility of nationalizing electricity. When these two former combatants of the anti-Duplessis movement discussed the best ways to defend Quebec interests, did they see that they already tended, in the heat of debate, to stress their differences of opinion?

This strongly antagonistic dynamic would make Trudeau and Lévesque political giants, individually, but it would turn implacably against the collectivity from which they both sprang. This collectivity would choose them both, simultaneously, for they wanted—without doubt—what was best for Quebecers when they fought, without reaching agreement, on Quebec Power and Saguenay Power, those "power companies" so familiar to the French Canadians of the pre-1960s.

THE SELF-DESTRUCTIVE DYNAMIC

In New France, while the *coureurs de bois* were taking possession of the North American continent in the name of His "Very Christian" Majesty, Intendant Talon was organizing the colony on the two banks of the Saint Lawrence. (In Quebec, as elsewhere, the "inside"/ "outside" characteristics have always existed.) French Power and Quebec Nationalism were two means for the Quebec identity to assert itself. Quebecers understood this well. They voted provincially for Lévesque and federally for Trudeau, believing that that was the best way to defend their interests.

The challenge was great: overcome, at last, the Conquest. Nothing less. In the Quebec context, it was necessary to transfer most of the power to the francophone majority. In the Canadian context, this meant increasing francophone power within the federal administration and some provincial governments; moreover, it meant devolving to the Quebec government some of the responsibilities that stemmed from Quebec's specificity.

This was the spirit that prevailed over the beginnings of the Royal Commission on Bilingualism and Biculturalism—the Laurendeau-Dunton Commission—in the mid-1960s. Many believed that was the only true way to respond to the aspirations of Quebec and to reinforce the country of which it was a part. As could be predicted, some elements of English Canada were very reticent about this approach but, most importantly, many others revealed an astonishing reserve of good will...enough to nourish a certain sense of optimism.

It was soon apparent, however, that atavism still prevailed, stronger than had been believed. The Quebec elites had general difficulty managing power to the advantage of the collectivity they came from. Independently of the good intentions of individuals, the dynamic that came into existence between the internal and external sides of Quebec's self-assertion carried with it aspects of self-destruction that would, in the end, decrease the power controlled by the Quebecers. It must be recognized that this was basically the result of actions by Francophones.

The internal side, Quebec nationalism, submerged itself in the ideal of independence. It grew blind to the historical English component, the Canadian component, of the Quebec identity. This blindness could only weaken it. The external side, French Power, showed a profound alienation toward the old Canadien identity of 1760. Its action was focused on the maintenance of the fundamental effect of the Conquest: the negation of political powers stemming from Quebec's specificity. It was revealing that the two sides merged in the emphasis they placed on "image": the bilingual image of Canada, the French image of Quebec.

Conciliation of these two sides, or of these two images, would prove impossible. French Power also represented the Canadian side; it alone carried almost the entire English element of the Quebec identity. Because this identity had only partially overcome the Conquest by the English, the other side had the best chances of taking over.

The major part of the effort of Franco-Canadian nationalism was aimed at increasing the powers of the State, which represented

Quebec's specificity on the political level. Contrary to what one would expect, the major consequence was not the strengthening of Quebec's powers, but the transformation of a Canadian political system that would favour the dilution of the Quebec identity within the Canadian identity. Once again, and at its own expense, the Quebec identity gave birth to an enriched Canadian identity.

The country's cultural duality was rooted in Canadian history and realities. It was invoked by Quebec nationalism to justify demands that would some day go as far as independence. For the majority of Canadians, that would mean the irremediable destruction of their country. This profound duality, never openly recognized as a result of the Conquest, had suffered its first important weakening at the end of the past century, during the colonization of Western Canada. In the heat of the battle between French Power and Quebec nationalism, this important source of Quebec's power was abandoned as a structural principle of the country. Cultural duality would be replaced officially by two less threatening (because they were more superficial) elements: bilingualism and multiculturalism.

Formal bilingualism of the federation increases the individual standing of all French-speaking Canadians, from the supporters of Quebec independence to the Francophones outside Quebec who have been almost completely assimilated. That is a sensitive issue for all descendants of Anciens Canadiens. Individually, bilingualism may become, too, a source of power for both Francophones and Anglophones who learn the other official language.

But not collectively. This is a paradox that says much about the Canadian and Quebec problem. Bilingualism does not generate power for Quebec, the only government controlled by Francophones, while it does for governments controlled by Anglophones. While Ottawa is keeping an eye on the application of the federal policy of bilingualism, the governments of the anglophone provinces are now responsible for the francophone minorities outside Quebec.

A good example of this situation was illustrated during the Meech Lake debate. In the new system, some English-Canadian premiers were permitted to justify their refusal to ratify the Accord by claiming—rightly or wrongly is not the point—that the agreement did not sufficiently recognize the rights of Francophones in their provinces. That was a major turnaround, if you remember that, in the era of French-Canadian nationalism, only Quebec felt responsible for the country's francophone minorities.

The second element that has replaced the duality of the official Canadian identity is multiculturalism. Contrary to what is sometimes believed in Quebec, this step was not taken to appease those in the West. Most of the human costs of assimilation had been paid long ago in that part of the country where this federal policy is often seen as another little-appreciated import from central Canada.

Multiculturalism was adopted for two reasons. It was to meet the needs of those immigrants who arrived in Ontario after World War II, whose assimilation was not yet complete. But it was also a means to avoid recognizing the country's biculturalism and admitting the political consequences of Quebec's specificity.

In principle, multiculturalism reduces the Quebec Fact to an ethnic phenomenon. Contrary to duality, this new aspect of the Canadian identity does not generate power for Quebec. By definition, the ethnic group is condemned to assimilation in the North American context.

Finally came the constitutionalization of a Charter of Rights, another layer of cement to hold Canada in place. In time, this Charter will create a series of individual rights related to the Canadian condition. The cost of that move was the American-style judicialization of the Canadian political system and a weakening of the country's federal character. That will affect, first and foremost, the province that has always had the most interest in maintaining federalism: Quebec.

The Charter deprives the governments of power, appreciably more on the provincial level than on the federal. In theory, it gives this power to the citizens via a judicial system controlled by Ottawa. The Supreme Court of Canada, whose judges are mostly non-Quebec Anglophones, was granted powers exercised in all sovereignty by the government of Quebec before 1982, in the sectors closely related to Quebec's specificity. Such as language. Fortunately for Quebec, some anglophone premiers obtained the provincial right to override the Charter in exceptional (in principle) circumstances. We'll come back to that.

It is not surprising that, in the process, Quebec lost the symbol of its political power of yesteryear: the veto. Quebec's power, as French Canada's representative, to prevent any constitutional modification was recognized *de facto* by English Canada.

This power was no longer compatible with the mutation of Canadian federalism, which implied a new weakening of the Canadian duality as well as the separation of French from the Quebec identity.

Paradoxically, the Canadian political elites represented the constitutional reforms of 1982, particularly the repatriation of the Constitution, as the reaching of adulthood by the country. And this despite the fact that the only government controlled by Francophones was absent and that Elizabeth II—a symbol of all the values that constituted the greatness of the British motherland—was kept as Head of State. It was clear that the integration of Quebec nationalism had failed and that the Canadian political culture, in its bilingual image, was still of Loyalist inspiration.

The constitutional integration of Quebec into the Canadian whole was accentuated. It was immediately clear that the Quebec problem would resurface sooner or later, worse than before. One of the reasons is that English Canadians' capital of good will toward Quebec would have been seriously drained. Individually, they often made considerable efforts to respond to what they were told their Québécois or francophone compatriots wanted.

It was by no means a coincidence that the transformation of the country took place under the direction of a Quebecer, Pierre Elliot Trudeau, whose nationalism had been transferred to the Canadian level. The country's need of Quebec, in order to exist, explains why English Canada finally accepted such unpopular and, according to some, unrealistic reforms.

English Canadians saw Mr. Trudeau as a Quebecer who expressed the true desires of his province of origin, while at the same time being Canadian, and as the saviour capable of casting out the demon of "separatism." However, he did not represent his Quebec compatriots on one fundamental issue: his first loyalty was to Canada while the majority of Quebecers identified themselves first with Quebec, although without rejecting Canada.

TRUDEAU NATIONALISM

Quebec nationalists were often given to underestimate, even to deny, the fact that Canada's former Prime Minister was first and foremost a Quebecer. This point of view is understandable. It reflects Pierre Elliot Trudeau's first loyalty to Canada and the ensuing consequences for Quebec. His whole past, though, is witness to the Quebec roots of a man who did not hide the fact that he would rather have been a dissident citizen of an independent Quebec than live in a Canada without Quebec.

Almost by definition, the Quebec identity comprises a more or less significant, more or less conscious, Canadian component. In the case of the leader of French Power, this Canadian content was predominant, but his identity was still very much Québécois; Quebecers who voted for Trudeau because "he is one of us" were well aware of this.

Mr. Trudeau was not only a Quebecer, he was also a nationalist. As strange as this may seem at first, we must place him in the line of the great nationalist leaders produced by Quebec in the past two hundred years. In this regard, he distinguished himself greatly from most Quebecers who worked in federal politics, content with being competent administrators. A good example is Louis Saint-Laurent, Canada's Prime Minister during the *Belle Epoque* of cooperative federalism in the 1950s.

Trudeau was a militant nationalist, tenaciously determined to change Canada, in light of what he considered to be Quebec's needs. Because of his charisma, Trudeau is often compared to Laurier, another French-Canadian Prime Minister, forgetting that Laurier was above all a pragmatist. Trudeau is as least as much like Henri Bourassa, who also demonstrated obstinate fervour for his vision of the country. Through his policy on bilingualism, Trudeau accomplished in his own way the old Bourassa dream of a binational Canada. Unfortunately, it was done on a superficial plane, that of the image... to the detriment of a reality that was no longer principally French Canadian, but Québécois.

Mr. Trudeau's political ideas were, in some major ways, divorced from the Quebec and Canadian reality of his time. His notions were imprinted with the seal of the idealism which has affected the Quebec elites since the Conquest. Trudeau had transferred his nationalism as a Quebecer to the Canadian level. This naturally led him to oppose a Quebec nationalism essentially centred, from 1962, on *la Belle Province*.

Trudeau, the theoretician, saw himself as anti-nationalist on principle. His political actions however, revealed a statesman above all preoccupied with the renewal of Canadian nationalism, based on elements drawn from Quebec nationalism. In retrospect, it is clear that his cold anti-nationalist generalizations were aimed at neutralizing only the Quebec variety of the phenomenon. Mr. Trudeau's relationship with Quebec nationalism was always passionate. His rejection, because it was without compromise, did little to hide the fact that he really was one of the family.

Under the cover of logical arguments that apply in principle to everyone, a political idea is always marked by subjective elements related to the proponent's personality. A perfectly bilingual Trudeau, then, gave birth to a system where bilingualism takes on at times the aura of a religion. Born of a francophone father and an anglophone mother, he presented—and still does—any political recognition of the effects of Quebec's specificity as a traumatizing breakup of the Canadian family.

THE REFERENDUM

It is difficult not to draw parallels between the Quebec nationalism that took flight in 1960 and the adventure of the Canadian Patriote nation at the beginning of the last century. The similarities between the two movements are too numerous to be coincidental. First, of course, both were similarly intense and lasted the same brief period of about thirty years. The two nationalisms also presented the same basically new characteristics, the furthest expression of the values of their respective eras: for Quebec nationalism, the generous idealism of the 1960s; for Canadian-Patriote nationalism, the universal thirst for equality and freedom provoked by the French Revolution.

Both movements failed in their attempts to achieve greater autonomy. In both cases, the nationalist elites proved incapable of correctly gauging the balance of the forces present; they also underestimated the consequences of a failure. They needed to see the Conquest as a simple accident on a journey, from which it was possible to return, ignoring the effects on the Canadien identity of 1830 and on the Quebec identity of 1980. One revealing fact: not enough of the population followed the elites in either case.

The Canadian political system was reorganized after these failures, based on the negation of the political power stemming from Quebec's specificity. In the nineteenth century, it was not until the Confederation of 1867 that part of the effects of the Union of 1840 were effaced. A modern equivalent could be an agreement such as that of Meech Lake, a reconsideration of the most dangerous consequences of the 1982 constitutional law.

All analogies have their limits. One of the differences between Canadian nationalism of the nineteenth century and modern Quebec nationalism is that the Patriotes could not learn any lesson from their past that would help them avoid defeat. Another important variation is that the lack of popular support was only one of the reasons for the failure of the 1837 rebellion, whereas it was the principal cause of the failure of the "Oui" vote in the 1980 referendum. In other words, the 1837 defeat was less predictable than that of 1980 because it was without precedent and was based on circumstances beyond the Patriotes' control.

The biggest handicap of Quebec nationalism was the opposite of what had originally been its strength: its newness, its desire to break away from the past—the French-Canadian past, the Canadien past—without first learning the lessons of former defeats. Besides, this process of prematurely rejecting emotionally trying events would continue, applying now to the Referendum itself.

For many Quebecers, the Referendum was an episode that was too painful to deal with: they simply moved on to something else. Ten years later, not only has there been no real assessment of this monumental failure, but it is even considered "passé" to refer to it.

Such an attitude is unfortunate. For, as long as there is no objective examination of the reasons for past defeats, Quebec will be more or less condemned to repeat the same mistakes, and often to inflict other failures on itself, each time moving further from the goal. It is uncomfortable to undertake this kind of collective assessment, and it is no wonder people have, until now, refused to confront certain realities.

People have been content to dodge the Referendum issue. One of the most frequent ploys in nationalist circles was to reproach Quebecers for having voted "Non" in a referendum when they "normally" should have voted "Oui," because "Non" meant saying "no" to themselves. Another popular explanation was to claim that the "Oui" would have had more of a chance to win if the question of independence had been posed more openly and if the Parti Québécois government had not been afraid of promoting sovereignty. Others accused the federal people of having unduly interfered in the referendum campaign. Finally, almost everyone agreed to denounce the shameful manner in which Mr. Trudeau, with the tacit support of

English Canada, distorted the meaning of the "Non."

Some of these reflections elicited ideas that were not altogether worthless. For example, that from the time it was decided to hold a referendum, it was not very advisable for Quebecers to vote "Non," in a Canada still built on the Conquest. Further proof of this reality was given when the meaning of the referendum's "Non" was immediately and shamefully distorted.

Many Quebecers felt betrayed along the way, when the solemn "I have understood you" of the pre-referendum was turned into a constitutional reform that diminished the powers of the only government controlled by Francophones. This vague yet profound feeling that something dishonest had happened, to the detriment of Quebec, is one of the explanations for modern-day Quebec's disenchantment with the federal Liberal Party.

Many people had difficulty emotionally integrating what had happened, which led them to put it aside and consider it not pertinent. Their excuse for this was a need for new realities, such as the economic power of Quebecers, the globalization of cultures, or a more open federal administration. Others, while still believing in the importance of a strong Quebec political power, gradually devalued the "Non" vote, as an accidental detour that they would eventually be able to negate with another referendum, to achieve independence.

It is revealing that the ideal of independence was never really questioned. It was only put off, set in parentheses, suspended, depoliticized. The diversity of the reactions failed to hide a common denominator. The people could not confront—and overcome—the fact that the referendum had represented a major objective failure for Quebec nationalism, much like the aborted Rebellion of 1837. People did not want to see that, just as 1837 could not have been stopped, some consequences of the Referendum could not be reversed.

It was probably about May, 1980, that Quebec nationalism had attained its peak, that its brute strength was at its highest. The Parti Québécois had proven that francophone power was competent in managing state affairs. In a universally or continentally privileged society, forty percent of Quebecers—one Francophone in two—were ready to take a true risk so that the Quebec identity would obtain the political recognition to which it had a right. Considering the ratio of power and the nature and substance of the Quebec identity, this percentage was enormous.

If Quebecers had been collectively capable of negotiating with the rest of the country between November 15, 1976, and May 20, 1980, a time when their strength was at its greatest...

But part of the Quebec identity desperately wanted to believe that things could go further, that it could return to a pre-Conquest state, cancel the event so to speak. The Referendum excercise had something deeply attractive about it, something that would obviate a cold examination of the chances of success and a measurement of the consequences of a failure. In itself it was the essence of sovereignty: the enjoyment of the right to self-determination.

These descendants of a people conquered by arms, people who had never felt fully responsible for themselves, were finally able to treat themselves to the satisfaction of being fully sovereign.

But the votes had to be counted immediately; strength turned to weakness. People soon realized that the price of the dream had been enormous. Too much of the energy that had been accumulated since the wiping out of the Patriots, one hundred and forty years earlier, had been burned off in just a few weeks. In one night. They had bet, on their own volition, on a battle they could not win.

Quebec nationalism had lost too much contact with the French-Canadian past to correctly evaluate the affective meaning of the words "Canada" and "Canadians" for many Quebecers. They had held on to, hidden away somewhere, the memory that in the beginning they were the Canadiens, and still were to a certain point. Most of these Quebecers would have preferred not to have to choose.

Since 1980, Quebec nationalism has not sufficiently acknowledged that Quebecers exercised their sovereign right to self-determination in that year, and chose to stay in Canada. In terms of political power, merely calling the referendum was a costly move. By once again putting the dream first, the people expose themselves to the definite victory of the distorted interpretation of the "Non" vote, constitutionalized in 1982. Quebecers mortgage their future, whatever that future may be, including an eventual independence.

The fact that any examination of the causes of the referendum defeat has been systematically avoided and that this defeat was underestimated, if not flatly denied, is not a good omen for the new Quebec Nationalism now developing. We have looked at some of the negative consequences of the withdrawal of French-Canadian Nationalism into religious messianism after the fruitless Rebellion of 1837. In the aftermath of the unsuccessful Referendum, there is a danger of repeating some aspects of this process.

Certain signs give rise to the fear that there is developing a modern version of the conservative Catholic nationalism that rendered nineteenth century French Canadians incapable of taking advantage of the political opportunities offered them after 1867. For 1989 is a little like 1842: Quebec is not even recognized as a distinct society...

But today's Franco-Americans have not yet left; you never know what new West is waiting to be conquered. Most importantly, Quebec society is still here, very much alive.

CHAPTER 5

From the Strength of the Image
To the Image of Strength

The proud Quebecer of today, reminded of this story, feels a rush of pity for the conquered people of 1760. It is not certain whether this feeling is entirely appropriate.

For the Anciens Canadiens—the terror of the American colonists of the time—were in some ways more powerful than those who have become their descendants. If they seemed more "conquered" than Quebecers, it is perhaps because they were less concerned with saving face.

When shedding a tear for the fate of their ancestors, Quebecers are crying a little, unknowingly, for themselves.

THE DISTINCT QUEBEC SOCIETY

The energy that French Canada of the pre-Quiet Revolution years invested in religious activities, and the spiritual mission adopted after 1840 to compensate for the fact that true power had escaped it, were transformed around 1960 into a political nationalism, based on the use of the powers of the Government of Quebec. The State succeeded the Church, as is well demonstrated by Quebec nationalism's slightly "civic religion" side.

One of the major effects of this state nationalism was the opening to Quebec Francophones of an economic sector that had been previously closed to them (with nuances that are of little importance here). The accelerated development of a competent public service and the creation of large, para-public, economic enterprises (such as Hydro-Québec and the *Caisse de dépôt*), enabled many of today's Quebec knights of capitalism to get their training.

Bill 101 released a francization process that gave the new entrepreneurs the operations base they couldn't do without. Throughout the Quebec territory, the traditional handicap of their Québécois identity and their francophone status worked to their advantage against competitors. The Quebec entrepreneurship talked about during these past few years is a direct result of Quebec's state nationalism; it could not have developed without Bill 101, one of whose most marked effects was economic.

The francization process operated at a deep level and in many areas. It is an error to reduce this process to its linguistic aspects and, especially, to the French image Quebec gave itself in 1977. Since the national phenomenon has a psychological nucleus, there is no doubt, however, that the fact Quebec, for the last ten years, has seen itself as exclusively French has considerably influenced the Quebec identity.

For the power of images has become paramount in this century. Since the Second World War in particular, it has become a key factor in the structuring of our societies. The ability to project an image carries with it political power—even though this power may be fragile when the image becomes too divorced from reality. Ronald Reagan's presidency of the United States is a recent example of both facets of this phenomenon.

Anyone can see that a new society has taken off in Quebec over the past thirty years—a society that has renewed its French roots, a society that sees itself as, and wants to be, French. It lives a little as if it were independent, even though its structural integration in the the rest of the country has paradoxically increased. Intellectuals who analyze their Quebec identity often speak of its American nature and of its ties to European values; they always emphasize its local roots. But they rarely say anything about Canada, which Quebec nationalism viscerally refuses to consider.

It sometimes seems as if Quebecers were able to take advantage of the effects of independence, without actually being independent. A Quebec woman, who moved to California in the 1950s and returns regularly to her province of birth, gave this caricature impression of the transformations: "You have become Frenchmen. You no longer speak as we did; you no longer live as we did. When I listen to a Quebec radio station, I feel as if I am in France."

Whether it is the way we tell time, the way Provigo displays "bulk goods" in its supermarkets, or simply in the general matter of taste, Quebec is more French than it was. In an infinite number of daily routines, the psychological cocoon of Bill 101 has enabled Quebecers to develop naturally their French side. Paradoxically, this is better described by the English term Frenchness than by its French equivalent *francité*. The French word brings out too strongly the intellectual aspect of a phenomenon that really is not that intellectual, since it affects all areas and social classes in one way or another.

In other respects, this type of evaluation should not be confused with any kind of neo-colonialism imported from France. The characteristic of today's Quebec identity is intrinsically one of a majority. This has simply permitted the development of something that has always been there and that makes Quebec society an authentic French society while very different from European French society. This evolution was encouraged by easier and more frequent contacts with a France that, since De Gaulle, has re-integrated the Quebec reality into its sphere of concerns.

Today's Quebecers are the descendants of French Canadians who, for generations, have had to accept the humiliation of a constant denial of their French character and their ability to speak their ancestors' language. French civilization coincided with one of the pinnacles of humanity, and the universality of the values it spread was not compatible with the status of a conquered people.

One of the most trying consequences of 1760 was incontestably the attempt to deny the French character of a Quebec identity that was vulnerable on this point; according to a classic psychological process, being abandoned by France could be experienced as a rejection, because they were "non-French." It is not surprising that today's Quebecers are particularly proud of their new French society and the image it projects. Neither is it surprising that they appreciate France's recognition of both their French character and its specificity.

The film, *The Decline of the American Empire*, did not star simple individuals, but rather an entire section of Quebec society. This production showed, by the ease with which the intellectuals in a large number of countries identified with the protagonists in the film, that there exists in Quebec an American society which is French-speaking and which shares many of its values with the rest of the Western World. At the same time, that did not prevent the society depicted in the film from being unmistakably Québécois, immediately recognizable, among other aspects, by its tone.

One of the most notable successes of Quebec nationalism was the widespread circulation of the "Québécois" label, which is often written in French in foreign texts. This label internationally broadcasts the existence, to those who understand these things, of a precise, although not always flattering, cultural content.

In 1977, the provisions of Bill 101 that imposed unilingual French public signs in Quebec surprised most nationalists, as well as making René Lévesque uncomfortable. The traditional demands on this issue were directed more toward a compulsory use of French everywhere—a French-first policy. After the initial surprise had passed, the people supported the prohibition of English signs, insisting that the message must be unequivocal if Quebec were to be made truly French.

Effectively, this section of Bill 101 was originally a show of force (using the power of the "image") intended to reverse a situation in which English was dominant. It was a means to affirm the fundamentally French side of Quebec. In any event, it would be only temporary. A stronger Quebec—an independent Quebec—would recognize the historic status of English as a Quebec language, while being less fearful that this would be the first step toward bilingualism and assimilation.

At first, francophone Quebecers were rather reluctant about the restriction of anglophone rights to post signs in their language. But they quickly became attached to this new French face. Something about it was eminently agreeable and it created a sense of self-worth for the Quebec identity. Then, with the Referendum defeated, temporary turned into permanent. The provisions of Bill 101 in regard to unilingual French signs became little by little a psychological substitute for the independence that had not arrived.

The powers of the Quebec government were decreased in 1982. Not only did the new Quebec society not benefit from any constitutional recognition, but it came up against a constitutionalized vision of the country that was incompatible with its own. In intellectual circles it has since become popular to place Quebec's specificity in doubt by reducing it to the French language alone. And, above all, it seemed as if English were infiltrating everywhere.

"The unthinkable" was showing the tip of its nose.

It was not surprising that Quebec needs more than ever to be French, or at least that its image remain exclusively French. What was originally, for the Quebec identity, the force of the image is transforming itself at times into the image of force, masking a weakness. The Quebec identity is weakening because it is losing contact with that part of itself it is no longer capable of seeing, because it is incompatible with the exclusively French image.

We've said that the political powers associated with the collective identity of the Anciens Canadiens came first and foremost from within, from their intrinsic strength, both before and after the Conquest. But the Canadiens of 1760 also took advantage of the strength of those British who believed it in their interests to identify with the conquered people. It was as a Canadien that Governor Murray, before returning to London, conveyed a portion of his conqueror's power to a Briand who had just been named Bishop. A part of the English Fact entered the orbit of the Anciens Canadiens, attracted by the considerable force of their roots and power of seduction. A sweet revenge (if you think about it) of the conquered over their conquerors.

This has become the other side of the systematic "siphoning" of the Quebec identity by the Canadien identity that we talked about earlier. For the process has continued, and is continuing; throughout Quebec's history, a fraction of the English Fact has increased the power controlled by Francophones: from the French Party of the eighteenth century to the judgments of the Privy Council of London, which enriched the originally modest powers of the Quebec government.

So, after 1960, Quebec nationalism was developed by the political actions of a government that owed a not-insignificant portion of its power to the interpretation of a British tribunal. And that does not include the case of those nationalists who found, at the heart of federal institutions, at the end of the 1950s, the intellectual freedom they had lacked during the Duplessis years. It was as a commentator on "Point de Mire," a Radio-Canada broadcast, that René Lévesque first made himself known.

Even if the Quebec population were entirely French-speaking, and even if Quebec were to become independent, the Quebec identity would always have this English component, this Canadian component that is not foreign to it. How many unilingual Francophones, on their first visit to Europe, have been surprised to sometimes feel more at ease in London than in Paris, because of mundane things like bacon and eggs for breakfast, lounge-bars in small-town hotels, and ketchup? Because of the manners and lifestyle Quebecers have borrowed from the English over the years.

This is the reverse of the French side mentioned earlier, but the Quebec identity is not as proud of it. Beyond recognition of the strictly Anglo-Quebec reality, Quebec society's need to see itself as solely French leads to the denial of a part of the Quebec identity by the Francophones themselves. An example is the vague desire to "presidentialize," in artificial fashion, " à la française," a parliamentary system dating back to 1791, which is not any less Québécois because it is British-inspired.

This situation also prevents Francophones from taking advantage of the ability of those non-Francophones who contribute to Quebec society and who are capable of reinforcing it. The refusal to recognize the anglo-Quebec community as such, and the need to consider it as one cultural community among others, denies reality and takes no account of history. Most of all, it throws out of Quebec society a number of Anglophones who had been precious allies of Quebec nationalism.

The situation of Anglo-Quebecers before the Quiet Revolution was so privileged that today, even after all of the reforms of Quebec nationalism, it still enjoys rights, institutions, and services that would make almost any other world minority green with envy. That this has been said so often as to become a cliché, takes nothing from the reality of the observation.

Besides, this community still enjoys privileges that are clearly derived from the Conquest. An example is the fact that the English versions of Quebec laws are on exactly the same footing as the French versions: a bilingualism imposed by the Canadian constitution at the highest level of the State; an institutional bilingualism that Quebec cannot reject. An eloquent symbol ...

There is one thing, however, that the anglo-Quebec community has lost and should be able to find in Quebec, in a Canada that would be no longer based on the Conquest: recognition. Recognition that it exists, that it has its place, even if this cannot be on an equal footing with the francophone majority. Even Anglo-Quebecers who are the most sympathetic to Quebec nationalism have difficulty admitting that their language and contribution are not recognized. This is particularly true if they are Quebec-born.

More and more, these Anglo-Quebecers will tend to identify themselves as simply Canadians, as opposed—in the strongest sense of the word—to the majority of Franco-Quebecers who identify themselves above all as Quebecers. French Quebec can only lose by this, because the anglophone community has important support in the rest of the country—within an Anglo-Canadian majority that has powerful means to thwart Quebec's just aspirations.

This dysfunction not only implicates the Anglophones proper. It also concerns those immigrants that Bill 101 wanted to integrate into the Quebec Fact by, among other things, imposing on them French-language schooling. Within these cultural communities, most students now learn French; they are more a part of the collective life of Quebec than their elders; from time to time, they watch French television and read certain newspapers. But that does not stop them, in almost all cases, from learning and using English; and they often feel more Canadian than Québécois. Even those who become very "French" are generally less affected by the psychological aftermath of the Conquest.

It is only normal to insist that immigrants and non-francophones in general learn French and take part fully in Quebec life. But, it is illusory to ask them to unlearn English or to behave like the descendants of the sixty-three thousand conquered Habitants of 1760. Yet that is sometimes what they are asked to do, implicitly, so that they may be considered true members of Quebec society.

Successful integration of these allophones into Quebec society forces the Québécois by origin to confront the reality of the English influence that these immigrants bring with them. The resulting paradox is that, in some francophone communities, there is more fear of being assimilated today than when the immigrants were totally anglicized. As if Quebecers are too weak to face the consequences of their own success.

English is a deeply ambivalent and perturbing element of the Quebec identity: at the same time both friend and foe, a part of ourselves that makes us stronger and the conqueror that wants our blood. But there is no doubt...the English is there. It is not easy to distinguish between Carleton, the friend of the Anciens Canadiens, and the same person who later, under the name Lord Dorchester, worked only in the interests of the Loyalists. That could be two sides of the same individual, two columnists of the same newspaper. One only wants, beneath his eloquent words, to prolong the Conquest; the other simply does not understand why he is refused recognition as a member of Quebec society.

In some cases, the "bad English conqueror[1]" may be a particularly colonized Francophone, and the "good English" may be unilingual English Canadians, such as that friend of the Québécois—in spite of himself—Manitoba's Premier Sterling Lyon. He was the one, not the Quebec government, who insisted, in 1981, that the new constitutional Charter of Rights include the famous "notwithstanding" clause. Unknowingly, this Winnipeg politician was helping to build Quebec society's only constitutional shelter to date.

We said that, in Canada, the concept of multiculturalism was used to avoid admitting the political consequences of Quebec's specificity by attempting to reduce it to its ethnic aspects. It is revealing to note that Quebec uses multiculturalism in an analogous aim, to relegate the Anglo-Quebec community to the status of one cultural community among others. The difficulty for the Quebec identity of recognizing its English component is the perfect parallel of Canada's refusal to politically recognize the Quebec specificity from which it draws sustenance.

It appears as though Quebec's exclusive French image is the last wall that is preventing some of the unsettled after-effects of the 1760 Conquest from surfacing in the modern Quebec identity. That is not insignificant. The emergence of English in the image projected by Quebec would cause the Anciens Canadians' descendants to relive some aspects of the original traumatism that were avoided during the eighteenth century because of the embryonic character of the collective identity of the Anciens Canadiens.

It has been felt for some years that any toning down of the province's French face would be explosive. As soon as this face seems threatened, anxiety increases. Any sign of English would create unexpected reactions from many Quebecers, even from many of those who agree in principle that English signs be permitted. The rising of a fear never really confronted: "There, just what we've always been afraid of—

'the unthinkable'—is finally coming."

It is important that Anglo-Quebecers be aware of this reality; and so should all Canadians who think that the prohibition of English signs is simply a demonstration of intolerance.

BILINGUALISM BENEATH A FRENCH IMAGE

Nonetheless, it is important that Quebecers be aware of the price they will probably have to pay for the undeniable psychological satisfaction of an exclusively French face in Quebec. It's already significant that, since the French face had become untouchable, the government has opted for its integral maintenance, while opening up more to the principle of recognizing English inside commercial establishments.

By placing too much emphasis on the face, on the form, we let the substance become more English and the reality more bilingual, in fact, if not in law. For Anglo-Quebecers, and some Francophones, will have a natural tendency to compensate for the official nonrecognition of their language by posting more English inside than there would normally be needed. Already, in the days that followed Quebec's decision to invoke the "notwithstanding" clause to protect the French face of Quebec, when anglophone ministers resigned emotionally and noisily, it was impossible not to see the unexpected importance of the anglophone reality, just as, paradoxically, it had been refused the right to show itself. As if the less we were willing to see the English fact, the more power it was given.

In time, this should normally result in a more systematic bilingualism, not in signs, but in daily life. The "bilingualization" of a Quebec reality that has always been fundamentally French represents the true danger. In the Quebec context, placing the two languages on equal footing is the best guarantee of an accelerated assimilation.

The Quebec reality, which is in essence French, has an English component. In the 1970s, French Power and the Parti Québécois gave substance to the idea that we must choose between French-English bilingualism or French unilingualism. The Quebecers of the year 2000 may find themselves with the worse option of the two: integral bilingualism behind a unilingual French face. Unless there is total French unilingualism, most nationalists would prefer that solution to the other... accept the English that is there, but control it.

Emotionally, that would be more difficult: Quebecers would lose a little face and confront the old French-Canadian shame still concealed within the proud Quebec identity. It would mean knowing in advance that there would be mistakes and that the Anglophones, given an inch, would next day want a yard: bilingualism, free choice. Perhaps there would be more Francophones than you would expect who would post signs "in both languages" and, who knows, in English only. That would open the floodgates without being entirely certain that they could be closed.

That would be confronting "the unthinkable."

So, as Quebecers, it would be necessary to manage power as it has rarely been done before...collectively and individually. This could be accomplished by firmly stopping the process at just the right time, despite protests from almost everybody, and notwithstanding all the fine charters. Under the disapproving eye of the English, Quebecers would have to assert, without yielding, the legitimate power that flows from Quebec's specificity. They would have to become their own conquerors.

Will it come to that one day? Is it possible? For the time being, in any case, it is unthinkable.

QUEBEC SOCIETY WITHIN CANADA

Slowly but regularly, the weight of Quebec in Canada has been diminishing for the past twenty-five years. Although during the first century following Confederation Quebec made up thirty percent of the Canadian population, this percentage was approximately twenty-five percent in 1981. And the powers of the Quebec government were weakened by the constitutional reform of 1982.

Many Canadians and Quebecers, however, will still refute the reality of this Quebec regression. They will cite, of course, the economic dynamism resulting from Quebec's new entrepreneurship, the envy of the rest of the country. They will underline the fact that it has become almost an unwritten rule of Canadian politics that the Prime Minister hail from Quebec. Finally, they will remind us that the province's political power on the national scene has never been stronger than since the election in the fall of 1988. This is because structural changes such as those of 1982, which affect the nature of a country, take time to produce an effect. It is also because the Quebec identity is often confused these days, in Quebec as in the rest of Canada, with its preferred defense mechanism: the French image.

Well, from one ocean to the other, Canada is presenting a bilingual image that is stronger than ever, while in Quebec, for the first time since 1760, the official image is exclusively French. If one sticks to the image, not only is Quebec sovereign, but it has succeeded in partially annexing Canada. But, this image is evidently misleading because, in Canada just as much as in Quebec, one of the principal effects of the reforms of French Power and Bill 101 was the separation of French from the Quebec identity with which it was traditionally associated. Quebecers lost their exclusive right of ownership of French.

It should not be forgotten that the country's bilingual image is not devoid of importance for the Quebec identity which is, in part, a secret Canadian identity. Through bilingualism, Quebecers are recognized all over Canada as French, equal with English; while there still lies that buried conviction of having been rejected by France and conquered by the English. When Canada's bilingual image erodes, which happens frequently, a feeling of hurt comes out most often in Quebecers.

Because of the dysfunction resulting from the Conquest, this need of an image was pushed very far and in opposite directions. An exclusively French Quebec, a bilingual rest of the country...To the casual observer, Quebecers appear incoherent and unreasonable, their need of an image out of proportion with their strength. But, it is precisely because the loss of powers (to Canada's advantage) was appreciable that Quebecers' need of an image is so strong.

If Quebec's power is slowly regressing, if at times it is overestimated, there is no doubt that it is still a major force in the system. The same is true of the Quebec identity, whose dynamism continues to assert itself here and there in an array of sectors. In a 1988 example, the ratings of French television improved, to the detriment of anglophone channels. Yet, given that the progression of individual bilingualism and the development of cable distribution make English television more accessible throughout the province, improved ratings for anglophone channels were considered inevitable.

Paradoxically, this vitality becomes a problem when the integration of Quebec increases... within a Canada that does not recognize the source of its strength: Quebec's specificity. The dynamic of confrontation inherited from the Trudeau-Lévesque era is there, encrusted in the hearts of the Quebec and Canadian identities.

CHAPTER 6

Assimilation

If you visit Lowell, a middle-sized city like so many others near Boston, consider yourself lucky if you run into someone near the Centralville quarter who still speaks French. That is where, in the 1930s, seven year-old "Ti-Jean" Kerouac, having just moved for the sixth time, began his tragic destiny as a Franco-American nomad.

The streets are still called Beaulieu or Boisvert; "Ecole Saint-Louis" is still engraved in large letters in the cornerstone of the local High School. Lowell's Franco-Americans settled in Centralville, when they were wealthy enough to leave *Little Canada*, on the other side of the Merrimack River.

There, between the train station and the factories, the French Canadians who got off the train from Montreal built, from 1880 on, what they affectionately called their "Petit Canada." Crammed into one square mile in five- and six-storey apartment houses, which often stretched the length of a city block, they lived among themselves for decades, in French, reading their papers and telling the old stories from "the Canada above."

Today all that remains of this area of Lowell is a large, undefined plot. A commemorative plaque is a reminder of the supressed sobs of those who were there in the 1960s when bulldozers leveled the last Tenement Buildings in the name of urban renovation: "We will never forget your…"

During the same period, depression and alcohol finally got the best of Jack Kerouac, who had become a great American writer.

The large Saint-Jean Baptiste church in the Little Canada of Lowell is still standing: "the ponderous Chartres Cathedral of the slums,[2]" as Kerouac once called it. The new parishioners speak Spanish. Next door, on Market Street, is an odd decoration: a huge fresco of Quebec City, as seen from the Lévis ferry; and, below a dreamlike

Chateau Frontenac, the inscription: "Bonjour! It's warmer in Quebec."
That is all that appears to remain of the Franco-Americans of Lowell...the shadow of the great Jack, of course, and the memory, somewhere, that it was warmer in Quebec.

THE FRANCO-AMERICANS

It is not by mere coincidence that the Franco-Americans have recently flooded into the collective consciousness of the Québécois. Cinema has seized the opportunity, creating a public saga; young rockers are writing beautiful songs about the great Jack. After the break of 1960, it's as though there has been a need to remember that the Franco-Americans were part of the family. There is a fear that what happened to them might happen to Quebecers, that the Canada above may follow the Canada below into the great funnel.

Assimilation: the flip-side of "the survival." More present than ever, that is the great fear in the heart of the Quebec identity. If you know anything at all about the subject, it is easy to understand the Quebecers' fear of assimilation, because it is based on fact. English Canada and the North American continent are full of former French Canadiens who no longer speak French: they make up nearly half the descendants of the Anciens Canadiens of the eighteenth century.

Many Canadians, many Anglo-Quebecers, sympathize sincerely with Francophones on this subject. But they cannot feel the incredulity, the rejection, the anger—and, at times, the beginning of hatred—of the Quebecer who believes that his right to the only place in the world where he is truly at home is being disputed and that its disappearance is in the cards. Sometimes it only takes one English sign.

This is the constantly renewed version of "the unthinkable," the overflowing repression of emotion passed from father to son by the descendants of the conquered people of 1760. Several sound analyses of the Quebec problem, although their facts are unassailable, miss the essence of the issue because they underestimate this unavoidable emotional factor.

The process of assimilation could have begun on the psychological level, as early as the Conquest, to be accentuated by the Union after 1840. If they wished to flourish on the federal scene, the French-Canadian elite of the nineteenth century had to cringe. In a speech he gave in Toronto in 1886, Laurier went so far as to say: "I fully admit that the English language is bound to be the language of this country, and no man in his senses will deny it[2]."

The first weakening of Canadian duality occurred during the 1880s, when the English character of the West became irreversible. At the time, this didn't appear to create any substantial changes for a francophone population concentrated in very large majority in Quebec. But today it is clear that the country's dynamic must have been deeply modified. This condemned those Canadian Francophones who would live outside Quebec or the bordering territories to a slow but inescapable assimilation. The situation would have been different, obviously, if Quebec had not been the only province controlled by Francophones; and the Trudeau ideal of a bilingual Canada would have been more significant.

Today, the process of assimilation is progressing rapidly for those Francophones outside Quebec who do not live in the parts of Ontario and New Brunswick adjacent to it. They live mostly in English, despite admirable individual efforts and Canada's official mythology. The Acadian community, historically different from all other francophone groups in Canada, is truly an exception, but in large part, it is true, because its territory is adjacent to Quebec's.

The surprising aspect of the century that followed Confederation is not the francophones' assimilation but, on the contrary, that their proportion of the Canadian population remained so stable: at around thirty percent. And that was in spite of the hundreds of thousands of French Canadians who exiled themselves to the United States, while the English were reinforced by an even greater number of European immigrants in the early twentieth century.

During the past twenty-five years, people have frequently gloated over the exceptionally high birth rate among early French Canadians— the highest, it was said, in the history of the white race. That, however, was a strong demonstration of the vitality of the French-Canadian identity. Even then, that only succeeded in maintaining the Francophones' position in the country; because the hemorrhage had begun.

The major cause of the Francophones' assimilation in the first century after Confederation was what happened in the United States, not in Canada. The French Canadians who left to earn a living in the south emigrated to a country where they would have no collective political rights, and where they would be treated as an ethnic group. Once again, the move did not change a great deal at first. To a certain degree, it was even thought of as advantageous; French Canada's territory was expanding.

For, in the beginning, the Franco-Americans proved pessimistic forecasts wrong; they continued to speak French and to feel like French Canadians for much longer than anticipated. To "the Canada above" of Quebec was added "the Canada below" of New England. The social history of this period abounds with accounts of these French Canadians commuting between the two Canadas to study, work, or simply visit relatives. Honoré Beaugrand, twice mayor of Montreal in the 1880s, had lived in Falls Rivers, Massachusetts, for many years. Calixa Lavallée, composer of "O Canada," ended his days in Boston.

The Franco-Americans' desire, constantly affirmed, to keep their identity and their emotional fidelity to their roots led some to believe that the Canada below did have a future. Some even went so far as to dream of the francisization of one or two American states, and New England's partial annexation to Quebec.

It was not until after World War I that the inevitability of French assimilation began to show itself. The *coup de grace* would be the social upheaval caused by World War II. That would particularly weaken the parish structures, which had ensured the survival of the Franco-American society for eighty years. In the 60s, an improvement in the status of ethnic identities in the United States affected the Americans of French-Canadian origin. You could no longer speak, however, of a Franco-American society.

THE FRANCO-AMERICAN LEGACY

The firmly rooted nature and tenacity of the old French-Canadian identity made it a great deal different from an ethnic identity. Unfortunately, those characteristics worked against the Franco-Americans because, in the American context, they could only be treated as members of an ethnic group.

They believed themselves the proud descendants of those who had discovered the continent; but they quickly learned that they were those not very smart Canucks who took longer than anyone else to climb the ladder of American success. This was because of that something in them that made them resist assimilation more than the other immigrants with whom they were in competition. In their Little Canadas, Franco-Americans remained, for a long time, Quebecers in exile.

This fidelity enabled Quebec to recover about half of those who had left before 1900. But that made assimilation more difficult for those who did not return, leaving bad memories that future generations would often prefer to forget. There was little French-European immigration to

New England; it was the French Canadians above all who came to make a living in the textile industry. Yet, the 1980 census reveals 813,199 New England Americans who claim to be of French origin: only 269,190 (less than a quarter of the total) "admitted" to being of French-Canadian descent[3].

This skinned-alive side of the Franco-American experience[4] should force those Quebecers who underestimate the human cost of an eventual assimilation to have second thoughts. You could present assimilation as inevitable, even desirable, if you overlooked this crucial fact: after a certain point, the non-ethnic aspects of Quebecers' collective identity would turn implacably against them. Perhaps the process has already begun.

It would be unfortunate, however, if the only thing Quebecers learned from the Franco-Americans' experience (as seems to be the case) were an even more visceral fear of assimilation and the need to fight, again and again, for their survival. The history of French Canada abounds in these emotion-filled appeals, unfortunately to little effect. If only so that the sad fate of their Franco-American cousins has not been in vain, the real, hard-earned lesson must be remembered. Good will, enthusiasm, and even legitimate rights are not enough; engraving French on the cornerstones of Lowell, or elsewhere, is futile if there is no longer the control of political power.

It is revealing to note that, in the beginning, and in the case of Franco-Americans and Francophones outside Quebec, a large portion of the political power of the old French-Canadian nation was lost. That was the requisite for an assimilation which, at the time, was not obvious at all. Later, individuals would fight against it, often with the energy of despair.

It is not surprising that the tendency of the Quebec identity to lose a part of the power based on its specificity is its real problem on the political level. One cannot help but wonder about the 1982 decrease in the powers of the only government controlled by Francophones, as a result of the Francophones' own actions. In the same light, the fact that the nationalist elites underestimated the stakes of the Meech Lake Accord and the priority given to the French image (at the expense of powers associated with the Quebec identity) are signs of a disturbing lack of lucidity and foresight.

The Franco-American adventure should also make one wary of official mythologies that do not stand up to the facts. A bilingual Canada, from St. John's to Whitehorse, is a dream; a totally French Quebec of Bill 101 is an image. The undeniable fact that remains is that the descendants of the Canadiens of 1760 have survived especially because they were grouped in one territory and they controlled a government, institutions, and businesses.

It would be just as bad to go to the other extreme, by not recognizing that the Quebecers' situation differs from that of the Franco-Americans. Deeply rooted in a territory where they form the great majority of the population, Quebecers control a government with important powers. French benefits from constitutional recognition in Canada. Quebecers have the strength of those who are in their own home. Even in the most pessimistic scenarios, they could never be treated, in certain major respects, as members of an ethnic community.

But we mustn't confuse the time nor the war. The Quebec phenomenon is unique. It is something between a full-fledged nation and an ethnic group. While modern Quebec nationalism was pushing in the direction of nationhood, the tremendous dynamic of North America pushes it toward ethnicity. In a Canadian constitution that solemnly proclaims the virtues of multiculturalism, that is, ethnicity, no one breathes a word about the distinct Quebec society. In North America, where law has replaced war, constitutional rules represent the ultimate power. They have a very strong structuring effect on the societies they govern.

Finally, the Franco-American experience should serve Quebecers as a lesson on the American mirage. It is revealing that the French Canadians who migrated to the United States were assimilated much more easily and completely than those, although less numerous and more dispersed, who opted to stay in Canada. This is because the American identity is much more vigorous than the English-Canadian identity, or the Canadian identity, period. There has never been a Canadian equivalent of the American Dream which, at the end of the millenium, affects almost every inhabitant of the planet.

Spontaneously, Quebecers frequently feel more at ease in the United States than in English Canada. Quebec nationalism's emotional refusal of a Canada based on the Conquest is eminently understandable. Yet, this refusal has an element of the suicidal when it is accompanied by a clear-cut "Americamania."

Imagine what Quebec would have become if annexation to the United States—Papineau's ultimate dream—had been realized. The old French-language colony of Madawaska, divided equally between New Brunswick and Maine in the 1830s, sheds some light on this hypothesis. One side of the river became American, the other remained Canadian.

Today's Quebecer will be surprised to find that most of the signs in Edmundston, New Brunswick, are bilingual, even if the population speaks French almost everywhere. This situation will bring back for older visitors the bad memories of the "French-Canadian Quebec" of days gone by. Just across the river, in Madawaska, Maine, the same Quebecer will be happy to recognize he is in the United States. The signs are in English; everyone speaks English in public; life is American. The casual visitor will leave without realizing that there was a time when, on both sides of the river, Francophones were the totality of a population which later received few immigrants.

History has given us ample proof that the Quebec identity benefited from the maintenance of a politically operational Canada. In this context, the Quebec elites' recent support for free trade with the United States, which, contrasted with the reluctance of a part of the population, was somewhat suspect—not in itself, but because it was almost unanimous and unreserved.

It seems that the inconveniences of all kinds that would have resulted from a Canada-Quebec rejection of free trade would have been worse than those that came with the signing of the Canadian-American treaty. The Free Trade Agreement, on the other hand, should open up interesting opportunities for Quebec's new capitalism as well as permitting major sales of electricity to the Americans.

The treaty, however, will inevitably increase North American "continentalism" and will have political ramifications. It is naive to believe, then, what has been repeated so often: that Quebecers, because of their language, will be less affected by this agreement than other Canadians. The effects will be quite simply different—and not necessarily better, if we consider the adventure of the Franco-Americans.

Some would claim, more or less consciously, that Quebec society was less critical of Free Trade than it should have been, because it was a good way to shun a Canada that does not recognize Quebec's specificity. "Independence via free trade" is too similar to the disastrous "independence à la carte" (which we'll discuss later) not to raise the spectre of another fool's bargain.

The phenomenon not only influenced the political side of nationalism, it visibly affected Quebec's new capitalism. By moving into the economic sector, nationalism has retained some of its basic characteristics, such as an unrealistic view of the long-term consequences of its actions.

This free trade issue has demonstrated how the after-effects of the Conquest weakened both Quebec and Canada. To some English-Canadian nationalists, Quebec's support of free trade had the appearance of treason; this made many of them reconsider their support for the recognition of Quebec as a distinct society. They were deceived by

Quebecers, in the same way as Carleton, who was surprised that the newly conquered Anciens Canadiens would not take up arms against the American invaders.

They don't want to see that this insistence on prolonging the effects of the Conquest and this refusal to admit the natural political consequences of Quebec's specificity, feed Quebec nationalism's visceral aversion to Canada, preventing this nationalism from recognizing its own community of interest with anglophone nationalism and from playing its role of watchdog over the interests of the Quebec identity ... and the Canadian.

The theoretical outcome of the process would result in absolute catastrophe for the two identities: annexation *de facto* , if not *de jure*, to the United States.

THE PSYCHOLOGICAL BORDER

Beyond some Quebecers' fears of ending up like the Franco-Americans, what is it exactly that threatens them? More than becoming a minority, or losing their culture, or being assimilated, the sword of Damocles hanging over the Quebec identity could very well be "folklorization."

The danger for francophone Montrealers is no longer that they will become a minority, as was feared in the 1960s when the anglicization of the Italians of Saint-Leonard became a cause celebre of Quebec nationalism. Even in the most pessimistic circumstances, everything leads us to believe that Quebec will remain overwhelmingly French. Francophones should maintain their majority position in Montreal and should even be able to improve it[5].

This contradicts the principal fear of many Quebecers who still fear that the wave of immigration in Montreal may tip the linguistic scale to the detriment of Francophones. There is obviously an understandable anxiety created by the low francophone birthrate. Besides which, the spectacular media coverage of the refugee problem sometimes gives the impression that the province is being invaded by foreigners.

We tend to forget that, if the birthrate is low, so is the net level of migration in comparison to other periods in history, such as the years following the Second World War. We also ignore the impact of interprovincial migrations. This benefits the Francophones, who tend not to leave their province as much as the Anglophones do. But, above all, there is the phenomenon already mentioned: francophone Montrealers are more in contact with immigrants than previously because Bill 101 is trying to integrate them into the majority. This increases the feeling of insecurity.

And what about the pet peeve of certain Quebec intellectuals: "acculturation"? This is a process by which one human community assimilates some of the cultural values of another. No one would deny that the acculturation of the Quebec identity, towards the values of the North America surrounding it, is more pronounced than it was in the time of the old French-Canadian identity. Some are worried about the scope of this phenomenon.

In reaction to this, some tend to consider the French language as the one truly distinctive trait of the Quebec identity. The paradox is that, in turn, this will emphasize the process of acculturation; the Quebec reality will, in some cases, become an American reality merely translated into French. There is a vicious circle: the broader the scope of acculturation, the more the Quebec identity is reduced to the French language, thus increasing acculturation and collective insecurity.

The integration of one culture's values by another has annoying aspects, especially for the elites. This is not, however, the determining factor in the culture's eventual assimilation. To the contrary, this could be a demonstration of the culture's dynamism. It is not afraid of going elsewhere to find what it lacks at home, to become (or become again) competitive.

The notion that a national or ethnic identity is defined not by its content but by its borders is fundamental. The content can be changed appreciably without threatening the identity. An illustration of this reality is the case of Ireland. From the point of view of a Quebec nationalism based solely on language, it is inconceivable that Ireland would fight so ferociously, and in such difficult conditions, to obtain its independence from England; especially when the national language, Gaelic, has been replaced by English. On the other hand, Catholicism has maintained itself in Ireland as a distinctive element, whereas the Quebec identity abandoned this form of identification in the 1960s.

The aim here is not to deny the evidence, i.e. the importance of the French language for the Quebec identity. But, it is important to draw attention to the error we commit in confusing an identity with one of its elements, be it crucial or predominant. The national phenomenon is largely psychological. That which defines it, that which is essential for its survival, is not such and such a content but, rather, the psychological border between the members of one group and those who are not part of it ... between "us" and "them."

Well, Quebecers have obviously not lost the ability to use an "us" charged with emotion. Not only is the psychological border of the Quebec identity still well defined but it is growing clearer, to compensate for excessive acculturation among other things. The modern Quebec Fact sees itself more separated from its environment than was the case for the former French-Canadian identity. By definition, the Quebec identity sees itself as that of the majority, while the French-Canadian identity lived at ease in an environment where it was that of a minority, whether in the United States, the rest of Canada, or even in Quebec itself.

Today's Quebecer is spontaneously sympathetic to Francophones outside Quebec. However, for him, it goes without saying that these people live in English Canada and are no longer a part of his universe, a universe that, since the Quiet Revolution, has become principally Québécois. From this separation came important differences between the two groups: one example is that Catholicism has remained an identifying element for Francophones outside Quebec, which is no longer really the case for the Québécois. On another level, Anglo-Quebecers are now an integral part of the Quebec universe, the proof being that some nationalists would like to francisize them, an approach which would have been incongruous for the French Canadians of the past.

The "frontier" concept explains why the French language has assumed such importance for the Quebec identity. It happened less because language was a principal defining element of this identity than because it was a container, a vehicle... a symbol. The linguistic regime and the French image serve to mark the territory and trace the boundary that the Quebec identity needs in order to maintain its integrity.

Nothing stimulates a national identity more than adversity. Threatened, this identity's absolute priority is to maintain its border. Sometimes, it has to rely almost exclusively on only one of its components, while it searches for other elements which will allow it to establish a more solid frontier. This is perhaps what has been happening to the Quebec identity, following the failed attempt to achieve independence and because of the lack of recognition of the political effects of a specificity that certainly includes the French language but is broader.

A concept such as that of the "distinct society," on condition that it generate political effects, would fortify a Quebec identity that, for the time being, is obliged to depend on the French language alone or on the most fragile element, the French image. It is noteworthy that French, although by far the most important element of Quebec's specificity, would very likely come out of the process stronger, not only in image but in real life.

Unfortunately, such a transformation would be unlikely to go smoothly. Apart from the "border" aspect, another factor explains why language has almost replaced the conscious Quebec identity. The projection of a uniquely French image is also seen as an independence substitute, a way to save face in the aftermath of the loss of powers resulting from the referendum failure. Joined with the bilingual image of Canada, this image protects the Quebec ego, more and more imperfectly, from waking up to certain permanent effects of the Conquest.

There is, incidently, a difference between the two mechanisms. In order for there to be a frontier, the linguistic regime in Quebec must be different from that in the rest of Canada—a systematic predominance of French without the forbidding of English, for example. The role as protector against the trauma of the Conquest is another matter. This requires that the image of Quebec be exclusively French and that the image of the rest of the country be bilingual.

There is still a big unknown, one that makes it difficult to foresee the future: the unique character of the Quebec identity, straddled between a full-fledged nation and an ethnic group. Numerous studies have been done on one theme or the other; you can relate to the Quebec reality certain concepts linked to them. But, invariably, there comes a time when nothing seems to work.

So you must come to terms with Quebec's solitude in the face of its destiny. That is its drama. That is its nobility. That is its opportunity.

STRUCTURAL INTEGRATION

Quebec has remained French, but its weight in Canada is diminishing. It has allowed the rest of the country to confiscate part of the power it had gained from its nationalist energy of the years 1960-1980. What is less obvious but more dangerous than acculturation is one of the consequences of the loss of political power: the strengthening of Quebec's structural integration within Canada. This is an objective factor of assimilation because it attacks the frontier which a national identity needs in order to survive.

Beneath the French image of Quebec and beneath the bilingual image of Canada, economic power is becoming more and more concentrated in Toronto, while a part of the political power has been transferred to English Canada. That means the insertion of a larger number of Francophones into networks where power is based on the Canadian identity and where progress and promotion take place in English. A new dynamic has been set in motion.

Ambitious Quebec Francophones now have their eyes on Toronto, Ottawa, or English Canada in general. These transfers, seen as temporary at the start, will be very much facilitated by the bilingual infrastructure bequeathed by French Power. This leads us to believe that, outside Quebec and its neighbouring zones, long-term assimilation is not inevitable. This is true on an individual level, but not on a collective level.

Francophone Quebecers who will live in English Canada, where the power is concentrated, will maintain frequent contacts with Quebec for professional and personal reasons. In time, they will naturally come to adopt, in regard to the distinctive aspects of the Quebec society, certain attitudes of the milieu in which they circulate. Since the values of the Quebec part of the system are hierarchically inferior, the Canadian values (i.e. principally English-Canadian values) are the ones that will be spread by the leaders of the networks referred to earlier.

Over the years, these perceptions will not fail to wash out onto the Quebecers who work in Quebec for those networks. In line with a classic process of alienation, everyone will tend gradually to consider Quebec's difference as a disparity that needs to be corrected in the Canadian context...even for the good of the Québécois.

This dynamic will be independent of the personal qualities of those who decide to work their way up to be leader of a network, not only through legitimate personal ambition, but because they are convinced that it is the best way to help the Quebec to which they are attached. And, in fact, their native province would not be any better served if they stayed powerless at home while non-Quebecers continued to exercise the available power.

These Quebecers are often competent and effective in their respective fields of activities. However, in regard to the Canada-Quebec dynamic, their actions could have a positive effect only in the measure to which they helped gain recognition of the political consequences of Quebec's specificity—on an individual or collective level. That wouldn't be guaranteed because, among other things, former Quebec nationalists have shown themselves the most implacable destroyers of the Quebec identity. Unconsciously or not, they transfer their nationalism to the Canadian level... like the system's inventor, Pierre Elliot Trudeau, who imposed his own law.

Most of these temporarily exiled Francophones will return to

Quebec. Some will bring in their luggage a touching but outdated vision of a Quebec identity. Others of these talented former Quebecers probably will stay in English Canada. Their children will become perfectly bilingual Ontarians. And then, with an assist from mixed marriages, most of their grandchildren will speak French as a second language.

More than minorization, acculturation, or assimilation, the threat to the Quebec identity is "folklorization." This could be accompanied by a progresssion of assimilation, without decreasing appreciably the proportion of Francophones in Quebec City or Montreal. The process still only slightly affects a Quebec identity that is very modern at the moment: the legacy of the Quiet Revolution. But the new dynamic is only just starting to work.

Unfortunately, Quebecers are not very wary of the structural integration and loss of powers associated with their collective identity. More often that not, they are not really aware of it. On the other hand, they are very much afraid of the disappearance of French. And you have the impression that the slightest breach in Quebec's French façade will mean a loss of power for the Quebec identity.

Fortunately, Quebec still holds a few good cards in a game that is not quite finished. It has the means to reverse some of the integration that normally should have occurred after the 1980 Referendum defeat and the constitutional changes of 1982. Politically, it regained a fraction of its lost power in the wake of the Supreme Court decision on Bill 101, which facilitates the use of the "notwithstanding" clause. Another major fact is that Canada will face a multiplication of inconveniences if it continues to deny the political consequences of Quebec's specificity.

Finally, Quebec's dynamism is incontestable on the economic level, a fact not without repercussions in numerous fields.

CHAPTER 7

Quebec's Management of Power

THE NEW ECONOMIC POWER

The increase in the existing institutional bilingualism and the placing of French and English on the same footing does not correspond to a Quebec reality which has always been essentially French. Moreover, in the geopolitical context of North America, this process has a somewhat suicidal aspect.

Comparisons with certain European countries do not take into account characteristics that are unique to Quebec: a small francophone collectivity at the heart of a continent preponderantly anglophone, which penetrates it deeply and in all areas. One should not underestimate the tendency of the North American environment to reduce the Quebec phenomenon to ethnic characteristics.

The individual bilingualism of a portion of the Quebec population is, in other respects, inevitable; at any rate, it does not have the same effects as institutional bilingualism. Some communities where two languages are used can remain stable for long periods. The case of Montreal itself is a good example. There has been only a little assimilation of Francophones in the Quebec metropolis, despite its long history of a high level of bilingualism[1].

The principal criterion for judging progression of linguistic assimilation in a community where two languages are used, telling us when we are in the presence of a linguistic transfer, is the use of one language in a field where, before, the other was used. In Quebec's case, according to how you look at the same reality, you will judge, in the light of this rule of thumb, that linguistic assimilation is progressing or that, on the contrary, the Quebec identity—including its predominant French aspect—grows stronger. The glass is half-full or half-empty, depending on how thirsty you are. That's a well-known fact.

The nationalist energy that French Canada used to invest in religious activities is now being exerted in the economic field. The action of the Quebec State, started during the Quiet Revolution, opened the way. In the 1960s, there was a transfer from religion to politics then, in the 1980s, a transfer from politics to economics. Quebecers who work in this new economic sector use English, because a large portion of the market is English-Canadian and American. But, they also work in French, because they are Francophones and their base of operations is of Quebec origin.

This is where the diagnosis depends on which end of the binoculars you're using to observe the phenomenon. Quebecers use English and French in the economic sector, which has replaced the religious activities of their French-Canadian ancestors as part of their identity. Those activities essentially took place in French. In this respect, it is obvious that Quebec has seen a progression of linguistic assimilation, from French unilingualism to French-English bilingualism.

We must state that not all the energy invested in religious activities has been transferred to economics, however. Since the Quiet Revolution, a considerable portion of that energy has continued to be exercised in politics. For this reason, the maintenance of the Quebec government's powers and the importance of gaining recognition for the political effects of Quebec's specificity are priorities.

It would be especially absurd to forget that religion and economics are two different domains. In the past, the economic sector was generally closed to Francophones. Everything took place in English. And again, unfortunately, the energy that used to be invested in religious messianism proved politically sterile. Now, for the first time, the economic field is truly open to Francophones, using in part their own language. Politically, that should prove more fertile than all the energy invested in the French language only in the old religious ideals.

This does not imply a negative judgment on the individual value of the religious ideals, sometimes admirable, of the French Canadians of the past. And it must be added that French Canada's missionary activity was not totally unproductive politically. It left some intellectual blueprints in Quebec and good memories in certain Third World countries, to the profit of today's Quebec entrepreneurs. The new Quebec capitalism's map of the world presents some troubling similarities with the geographic map of past French-Canadian missions.

The beginning of the 1980s was a time of rejoicing about Quebec's entrepreneurial boom; arriving in the nick of time to compensate for the loss of power by the government that had opened the door to it. The enthusiasm and aggressiveness of these new entrepreneurs raised many hopes in Quebec and succeeded in arousing the admiration, even envy, of the rest of the country. It did not take much more for some to realize that Quebec nationalism was dying. Politics were becoming a thing of the past. From now on it was: "Make way for the economy!"

We forgot, though, this evidence that has been proven a hundred times over the past two centuries: nationalism is a permanent feature of Quebecers' collective and individual lives, intimately linked to their geopolitical situation in North America. Far from being the prerogative of a political party or a social class, the phenomenon affects the whole of Quebec society, to varying degrees and in various forms. There will be no more nationalism in Quebec when there are no more Québécois.

It is now evident that Quebec's nationalist energy was simply transferred to the economic sector. This is one reason for the remarkable dynamism of francophone entrepreneurship over the past few years. The warlike reactions of the Quebec business world to the announcement of the coming move of the Quebec Nordiques was not the result of analyses of cold economic factors: it had all the fervour of the most classic form of nationalism.

Quebec entrepreneurs, aware of the ties between the new francophone capitalism and state nationalism, are worried about the weakening of the Quebec government's powers. They feel it is important to maintain the manoeuverability of the *Caisse de dépôt* on the stock market and to keep alive the possibility of a deregulation of financial institutions. Although these concerns have nothing to do with French as such, they will decide its long-term survival. The entrepreneurs have what it takes to fill the "empty shell of the distinct society," but they still need the shell.

For now, it must be said, the hopes invested in Quebec's economic nationalism are just that: hopes. The problem of the Quebec identity was never a lack of energy or enthusiasm. Quebecers have always been able to win big victories. The problem is that they have usually lost the last battle, the one that won the war.

Well, Quebec nationalism's true victory will not be to build, but to keep in Montreal an economic power that will spread throughout the country and the continent—while continuing to function to an important extent in French. There is no guarantee that the individual success of Quebec entrepreneurs may not end one day, because of takeovers, in the removal from Quebec of the leading corporations in the new francophone capitalism and in the relegation of French to an insignificant role in the companies which remain.

It would not be the first time that Quebec's nationalist energy was used for something other than the development of the distinct society that is the driving force behind it. Quebec's economic successes should not conceal the fact that, in North America, one can become an individual millionaire while at the same time being a member of an ethnic group in the advanced stages of assimilation.

Businesses will only stay in Quebec and continue to operate in French if it is not a handicap but, on the contrary, an advantage. In time, the risk of seeing Quebec's new economic power dissolve in the North American environment will increase, if the government does not have the constitutional means to oversee the economic and financial development of the distinct Quebec society.

Beyond this constitutional aspect, what will make the difference is the management of power by Quebec entrepreneurs for the benefit of their collectivity. Obviously, this will be true to the extent that they are not caught in individual "power trips" but recognize responsibilities toward the Quebec society that nurtured them. For the time being, that is not really the problem. Most of the time, the feeling of belonging to Quebec goes without saying. It is in this new francophone capitalism these days that we find all that is most vigorous in Quebec nationalism.

Economic power is still a power though…with all the risks it entails of dragging the anchor of the Quebec identity. Already, there are disquieting signs which lead one to believe that the new capitalism is not sufficiently realistic in regard to the long-term consequences of its actions for Quebec.

Are Quebec entrepreneurs overestimating their ability to protect the essential, the control of power, in an American environment where government policies will not systematically favour them, as they have in Quebec for the past twenty years? Do they tend too quickly to look down on the Canadian market and to not take full advantage of the fact that, in Canadian territory, they have more control over the political rules of the economic game?

Quebec nationalists mustn't play, on the economic field this time, the same game their ancestors lost one hundred years ago when all those French Canadians went to be assimilated in the United States, leaving the West to the Anglophones. There is no doubt more of a future than one would think for Quebec's economic nationalism in Canada—even from the point of view of a conquest of the American market.

THE VETO

What happened to the Quebec veto illustrated clearly the difficulty of the Quebec identity to manage power, as much on a collective as on an individual level. Weakened by the Referendum, the Government of Quebec on its own did not have enough strength to prevent the other Provinces and the Federal Government from patriating and modifying the Constitution, which they did in 1981-82, in spite of Quebec's opposition.

The legality of this initiative was later confirmed by the Supreme Court of Canada. In Quebec, as in English Canada, the Court's judgment was used as an excuse to declare that Quebec had never had the veto. Since one cannot lose what one has never had, or remove what has never existed, this reasoning obviously had the advantage of reducing challenges to the minimum. But this reasoning did not take into account the distinction between the juridical idea of "right" and the political concept of "power." A court establishes a right when it renders its judgment, but, even if the court is supreme, it cannot rewrite the political history of a country. It seems a historical reality that, until the 1980s, Quebec had enough strength to impede modifications to the Canadian Constitution without its consent.

It would be useless, though, to become involved in an emotion-charged debate on this issue, while leaving aside the truly important point. It is not that Quebec lost its veto, or even that its partners took it away; it is that the Quebec government of the period renounced, of its own accord, the principle of the veto that it at least thought it had. It had concluded that it was a case of a power that was too difficult to manage—in fact, of a power that was too great.

Claude Morin, at that time responsible for Quebec's constitutional negotiations, has often explained that the veto, somewhat the equivalent of the atomic bomb in international relations, was not that useful in the daily management of Quebec's relations with its partners. And again, in a Canadian intergovernmental system where premiers are brought to meet regularly and to form personal relationships, the Quebec premier who might have used the veto would have had the odious task of refusing his colleagues the change they unanimously desired.

The comparison to the nuclear bomb illustrates that the veto, like nuclear weapons, has a power of dissuasion. This brings out the fact that it was the mark, for Quebec, of high status, one of the highest short of independence itself. At the international level, countries that have nuclear arms enjoy a status that other nations do not, even if they are wealthier or more populated.

This status generates power in areas other than nuclear, but on one condition: the other countries must be convinced that the nuclear power will use its arms if its vital interests (the "essential national interests" of Kissinger) are at stake. Such determination is the essence itself of any power of dissuasion, whether we are speaking of the atomic bomb or the veto. Actual use of the weapon, far from being indispensable, demonstrates that its power has decreased because it had not been able to dissuade. Eventual use will always be difficult because, by definition, the power of dissuasion poses a disproportionate threat.

What would we think if France or the United States unilaterally renounced nuclear armament on the pretext that the eventual decision to send missiles would be too difficult for their presidents to make? We would think they had become weak. It is in this sense that the veto became too large a power for a Quebec identity torn between French Power and Quebec nationalism. It appeared as if, while dreaming of a slightly magical independence that would free it from the constraints of its geopolitical environment, the Quebec identity was becoming too weak simply to exercise the power it already had.

It was the determination that was lacking, as became evident when Quebec itself renounced the principle of the veto. One of the reasons invoked was the difficulty of the Premier of Quebec, before the disapproving gaze of his colleagues, of exercising the ultimate power of the collectivity he represented. That says a great deal about the Quebec identity. Anchored deep within it is the need for the approval of "the other," whether it is the Conqueror, the English, or the Canadian part of itself.

The rest is well known. Mr. Trudeau's constitutional reform had many drawbacks, but it did recognize Quebec's traditional veto. In a desperate attempt to gain the support of the other provinces and thus block the leader of the French Party, the government of the Parti Québécois traded the veto for the right to withdraw from any undesirable constitutional modification, with financial compensation. This power was less important and less troublesome for the rest of the country than the veto. It could not be applied to federal institutions, especially the House of Commons and the Senate, from which Quebec could not withdraw.

The paradox is that, although the Quebec government was hoping to exercise the supreme power of independence, it traded a less potent but real power for a power still less important. Quebec renounced the principle of the veto, the ability to exercise power over its partners. The problem was that the partners did not in the least, in return, renounce their control of Canada, of which Quebec was still an integral element.

Some made a point of stressing that the right to withdraw was an important gain for Quebec, a kind of "independence à la carte." There was, though, a fundamental difference between the right to withdraw and independence: Quebec stayed in Canada. Compared to the right to the veto, it now had even less power over that same Canada. Events would soon prove this point. Six years after the veto has gone for good, Quebec is still trying to obtain the financial compensation promised if it withdrew from a constitutional modification it did not want.

After the Referendum's "Non" vote, an alliance should have been formed between the two wings of Franco-Canadian nationalism, French Power and Québécois nationalism, in order for Quebec to conserve its right to veto. But such an alliance became impossible because of a fundamentally antagonistic dynamic. They were more concerned with wiping out the other party than with maintaining the power of the only government in Canada controlled by Francophones.

COLLECTIVE MANAGEMENT; INDIVIDUAL MANAGEMENT

The difficulty for a Quebec Premier, whoever he was, to exercise the veto led, then, to the renunciation of the principle of this power. That is definitely one of the situations where are interwoven the individual and collective aspects of an identity. As representative of the collectivity, the Premier could have chosen to use the veto against his partners; but he was also an individual, who found it arduous to assume that responsibility.

Obviously, this is not a typical example. It does have the advantage, though, of bringing out the links, the dynamic, that always are present between the collective and individual aspects of an identity like that of Quebec. A problem in management of power at the collective level must stem from—and have effects at—the individual level.

It was as an individual that the Premier of our example found it painfully difficult to use the veto against his partners. It is normal for the Quebec identity to be weaker in certain of its individual aspects than in its collective aspects. As in other areas, union creates strength. With the support of the group, for example, French may be decreed the language of work; an isolated individual obviously could not impose this in his own workplace without being called a fanatic.

In the case of the Premier, what is important definitively (beyond the soul-searching likely to be felt by any individual placed in the same situation) is that the occupant of this key position have the strength to use his government's veto against his partners, if he feels that the vital interests of the collectivity he represents are at stake. In other words, he must have the strength to withstand the disapproving glares from those on whom he imposes his will.

The problems start, for the Premier and for all Quebecers, when the gap betwen the collective and individual aspects of their identity becomes too wide. When the Premier can no longer find within his individual Québécois identity the determination which will allow him to affirm the collective power of Quebec. When Quebecers, in the variety of situations of modern life, cannot find in themselves as individuals the will to take advantage of the power generated by the collective aspects of their nationalism.

This seems to be what is happening to the Quebec identity. One of the reasons that Quebec renounced the veto principle was that it was personally difficult for its Premier to use. The same process takes place on the individual level for Quebecers in general. The power exists; that is not the problem. It is, rather, the difficulty of enforcing this power in the presence of the "English." So, it is lost... to the advantage of the latter.

These days, the same is true of one of the most important and most positive consequences of the combined action of French Power and Quebec nationalism: the increased knowledge of French among Anglophones. In the rest of the country, this phenomenon affects mostly the elites, as a result of the federal policy on bilingualism. In Quebec, the entire non-Francophone community has been affected by the francization policies.

Despite some harmful side effects, the federal policy on bilingualism was not merely a trick, as some Quebecers tend too readily to believe. Bilingualism has become a major component of the Canadian identity, one of the keys giving entry to the country's new governing class. The increase of bilingualism of the English-Canadian elites (to varying degrees) is a concrete reality, especially for the young. The ability of the English elites to understand French, although not necessarily to speak it, is greatly underestimated in Quebec.

Even though this is first and foremost an elitist phenomenon in the rest of the country, Francophones should recognize its advantages: an increased opportunity to use their mother-tongue in areas where the power is concentrated. The choice of which language to use is not an easy one in terms of the values and the points of reference it propagates. A conversation in French gives the advantage to those who are of a principally Quebecois identity. In Quebec, anglophone bilingualism is not only for the elites. The majority of non-francophone Quebecers are now bilingual, again especially among the younger generation.

The Anglophones' new-found ability to understand or speak French is a potential source of power for Quebecers. And yet, too many Quebec Francophones continue to communicate with Anglophones in English, despite the latter's ability to express themselves in French. There are even indications that this situation is becoming worse. The varied reasons given to justify such behaviour are often very sensible.

A certain reputable Quebec nationalist will automatically speak English in public as soon as he steps outside of Quebec, whether his listeners understand French or even if an appreciable part of the audience is Francophone; this is the application of the principle of dividing Canada into Quebec and the rest. Other Francophones, from the business world, in Quebec this time, are eager to speak the "language of the customer" to Anglo-Quebecers, who have approached them in French! A certain Quebec minister will often use English during formal intergovernmental conferences, despite the availability of a costly simultaneous translation system. That makes it easier to make "real contacts," he will argue.

Some will say that they simply want to improve their English; many simply will try their best to be polite toward their anglophone co-citizens; others, disgusted or apathetic, will bend to the growing number of Anglophones who refuse to speak French in Quebec. Everyone will insist that the most important thing is to be understood. So, English will be the immediate choice in mixed company, where it is taken for granted that almost none of the Anglophones understands French while all the Francophones—or almost—know English.

The reasons vary: the result is always the same. Once again, inside and outside Quebec, Francophones tend to speak English when there are Anglophones present, and French when they are among themselves. It is like the good old days of French Canada before the Quiet Revolution, when Francophones carried the full burden of bilingualism; except that Anglophones of that time almost never spoke French.

When we look at this situation from the point of view of power management, however, the result is clear: by speaking English, Quebecers are putting themselves in someone else's territory, where they are handicapped in comparison to their listeners. Even in the exceptional cases where they have mastered the language of Shakespeare. Canada and Quebec being what they are, this handicap is frequently unavoidable, and it can be compensated by other factors. Even if Quebecers do not always lose when they use English with Anglophones, it would be in their best interests to use French when they can, if they want to exercise their prerogative as Quebecers.

Incidentally, we should denounce the sophism of pretending that, in this type of situation, the most important thing, after all, is to be understood. That is the ultimate excuse, the one used most often, for turning to English. Even more important than being understood is to exercise your power and achieve your goals, still in the perspective of a maximum management of power. In some cases, not being fully understood can even be to your advantage, in so far as the one who does not understand has the disagreeable impression that he should.

By not annexing the psychological territory that could result from Anglophones' new-found competence in French, Quebecers are playing with fire. The conqueror side of the Canadian identity is lurking. Even today, it is well known that some English Canadians passing through the most francophone regions of Quebec speak spontaneously to the locals in English, without bothering to find out whether they speak the language. Toronto's *Globe and Mail*, "Canada's national newspaper," thinks it normal to have the only coin-operated newspaper dispensers on the streets of Quebec City, an entirely French city. Quebec newspapers only have to do the same, it seems…

Given this conqueror characteristic, the ability of the English-Canadian elites and Anglo-Quebecers to speak French may be only a passing phenomenon … lasting just long enough for the Anglo-Canadian majority to win part of the power that used to be associated with Quebec's collective identity. Bilingual Quebecers will continue to speak English with Anglophones, but they will have lost the satisfaction of knowing that they could have spoken French had they wanted to. As for unilingual French Quebecers (seven out of ten, in 1981), they will have no other choice but to learn English.

This relative overuse of English by Francophones may be explained by the fact that they do not feel it is a foreign language like the others; they have been exposed to it in many private or public situations. One could even wonder whether Quebecers are, unconsciously, using English more frequently in their daily life to compensate for keeping this taboo part of the Quebec identity hidden under a bushel.

But the real reason is a clear sequel of the Conquest, the other side of something Murray had already seen in the Anciens Canadiens: the sometimes excessive kindness of a people whose unofficial national hymn is "C'est a ton tour de te laisser parler d'amour." (It's your turn to let yourself speak of love.) At times, a Quebecer has difficulty asserting his power under the disapproving look of the English. It is not surprising that he reacts by wishing these same English—this threatening side of himself—would disappear.

Beyond the slogans, if Quebecers truly want to renew their nationalism, they will have to abandon this excessive kindness and harden their individual identities. This will be even more necessary for those who are not always at ease in English but who will make more and more contacts with Anglophones over the next few years. These Francophones should not limit themselves to learning English; they should also impose their mother tongue. That is a job where the State, be it Québécois or Canadian, can never replace individuals.

No one doubts that a vigorous nationalism, in these collective and political aspects, will always be essential for the blossoming of the Quebec identity. In order to be effective, this nationalism still has to keep in mind the nature of this identity. One of its main problems is its difficulty asserting its power under the eye of the "English"; it would be ill-advised to bet everything on a constitutional provision such as the "notwithstanding" clause, despite its undeniable force.

The principal after-effect of the Conquest on the Quebec identity is in its difficulty in maintaining the considerable power it generates. World history has amply demonstrated that it was not by chance that the English were victorious over the French in 1760. For as long as the Quebec identity does not appropriate what was then the English strength, for as long as it does not become its own conqueror, it will be condemned, unfortunately, to lose the same battle of the Plains of Abraham, over and over again.

This is a tremendous challenge: to stabilize the Quebec identity in relation to the Canadian identity. It is the psychological equivalent of independence, the conquest of the Conquest. So that Quebecers will finally begin to win again, for real.

Such a process could be made easier through awareness: the Quebec identity has an English component that it can control. The conquering power has potentially become its own. This fraction of the Quebec identity, at present perceived as a threat, could act like a vaccine, stopping rather than accentuating the process of assimilation into the great North American entity. But one still has to be able to exercise one's power in the presence of this English part without giving in to it, but also without denying it.

An independent Quebec would have been strong enough to recognize the historic status of English as a Quebec language. In turn, you might think, a Quebec that integrated its English component would regain the capability of achieving independence. Of course, if Canada were more accepted, this option might no longer be necessary or desirable. We should not underestimate, though, Quebec society's profound aspiration for self-determination, especially if the rest of the country does not grant it the recognition to which it has a right, and without which the survival of Canada goes against the interests of Quebecers.

A Quebec that better integrated its English component would manage its power better and be more able to negotiate a different relationship with the rest of the country.

CHAPTER 8

The Provinces and
the Regions of Canada

THE EXCESSES OF PROVINCIALISM

Under Prime Ministers Mackenzie King and Louis Saint-Laurent, the cooperative federalism of the 50s and 60s gave way to what was called "Nation Building[1]," the gradual centralization in Ottawa of the most important powers. The Quiet Revolution and the assertion of Quebec nationalism stopped this process in the 60s. During the 70s, the drive was reversed and we entered a period of "Province Building."

The anglophone provinces understood that they could profit from Quebecers' demands on Ottawa. This was true particularly of the provinces in the West, which, as quickly as possible, wanted to bank the political benefits of an unprecedented economic prosperity and put an end to the traditional alienation of this part of the country in relation to Central Canada.

The provincial governments of the West brought the operation to a successful conclusion, skillfully thwarting the plans of a Trudeau who was fundamentally a centralizer but was blinded by his vendetta against Quebec nationalism. The Constitution of 1982 adopted an amending formula preferred by all four Western governments. It was based on the principle of provincial equality, with no Quebec right of veto and no reference to the concept of regions.

It was a Pyrrhic victory, a confirmation that the country's provincialism was increasing; there would be no room for regionalism as a structural component of Canada. And yet, Western power within the Canadian whole would have been greater if the region had had the possibility to speak politically with one voice, at least in some circumstances. Historically, a government representing the West, or just the Prairies[2], would have carried more weight than the isolated provinces, in competition with one another. The West's weakness in relation to the region-provinces of Quebec and Ontario is similar to a divided Europe's handicap compared to continent-states like the United States or the Soviet Union.

Because British Columbia is separated from the rest of the country by the formidable barrier of the Rockies, it has always had a particular personality that makes it aspire to the status of a separate region, the Pacific. Over the years, the governments of the Prairie provinces have themselves acquired a certain legitimacy and competency. That is the result of a process that began as early as 1905.

In that year, Laurier decided to create two new provinces, Saskatchewan and Alberta, from the Northwest Territories. Because Manitoba already existed, that made three Prairie provinces. The Prime Minister did not create one large province in this part of the country, which would have been easy for him to do, because he did not want to threaten the political supremacy of Quebec and Ontario. Although he was often considered the Father of the West, he was also its evil genius, because the plan would prove successful.

In the beginning, Alberta and Saskatchewan were above all political creations whose bases in reality were weak[3]. You have only to glance at a map to understand that: the provinces' borders are almost perfectly geometrical. Until about the Second World War, the Prairies were a region, in the full sense of that term. Their citizens were united by common characteristics that separated them from other Canadians. They were immigrants, neither English nor French, often from Central Europe. Their economy was based on single-crop wheat farming. They were partial to radical and marginal politics like Social Credit or socialism. At one time, agricultural groups even created a regional form of political organization.

Inevitably, though, the territorial bases of governments have structural effects on the societies they govern. Having three provincial governments for the Prairies gradually led to the establishment of three provincial societies. The region's population naturally became organized on a provincial basis, whether economic, social, or cultural. In other words, provincial governments developed within themselves the societies they lacked at the beginning.

After the last war, the diversification of the region's economic base fed this evolution, putting the Western provinces in competition with each other. The birth of an Albertan economy based on energy resources drew that province closer to British Columbia and away from the still-rural province of Saskatchewan. Finally, the 70s saw the emergence of energetic and competent provincial administrations, especially in their way of dealing with Ottawa. The values and life styles of the inhabitants of large urban centers in the West now resemble those of their compatriots in Toronto and Halifax. Compared to the rest of the country, though, the Prairies' specificity is most evident in its rural characteristics.

The weakening of regional specificity in the West and rising provincialism are very closely related. They have become unavoidable factors of Canadian political life. It would be an exaggeration, though, to conclude that this part of Canada does not have its own regional concerns and frustrations. Contrary to Quebec, the West has never seriously considered leaving the country. Its ultimate goal is not even the increase of the powers of the provincial governments. Far from wanting to be an outsider, this region aspires to a more complete integratation into the system. It asks that federal policies seriously take into account its concerns.

It is not surprising that the Quebec performance of the past twenty years—a catastrophe of the first order in the optic of a Québécois nationalism based on the increase of Quebec's governmental power— appears to the West as a success to be envied. It is undeniable that structural changes were made to the Canadian system so that Quebec would be more integrated—poorly, but that is another problem—with the rest of the country. Federal policies are more concerned with Quebec's specific interests, as expressed by Quebec's French Power in matters of language. Yet, this is exactly what the West wants: to influence the central power in the sense of its own priorities, which are essentially economic.

How can one not admire a Quebec that has succeeded in bringing about a federal bilingualism policy that would apply in Regina, while at the same time declaring itself unilingually French? How can one not be angry with a province-region that has provided the country's Prime Minister for the past twenty years and whose block vote for the winning party ensures it a generous portion of federal power? How can one not be envious of the birth, in Montreal, of a vigorous economy controlled by Francophones and in accord with the interests of the Québécois?

If the West can with difficulty aspire to such successes, it is partially because Quebec nationalism is fed by its own energy, which is not regional in nature. Even without that, the region would be politically disadvantaged in relation to Quebec because of its "provincial corset." This would prevent it from harvesting all the political benefits that would naturally arise from its increase in population and wealth.

It must be said that the refusal to recognize the political consequences of Quebec's specificity—the principal result of the Conquest—
is about to carry Canadian provincialism to unequaled heights. By
definition, the interests of different provincial governments are not
always the same as those of the region of which they are a part.
Reinforcing provincialism, therefore, can only worsen the already existing regional alienation... not only to the detriment of the West and the
Atlantic, but also to that of the entire country.

It was partially because we did not want to accord any kind of
particular status to Quebec that, in 1982, we finally held to the principle
of equal provinces. We put aside the idea, which was originally
supported by many and which made good sense, that any amendment of
the constitution should include a regional aspect. The process
continues...with more and more perverse effects.

During negotiations that led to the Meech Lake Accord, all of the
provinces were finally awarded the right to veto modifications of federal
institutions such as the Senate. This was done, not because all the
provinces asked for it or needed it, but because the need to give this power
to Quebec was recognized. According to the Trudeau credo that still
dominated Canadian political thought, what was offered to Quebec
should also be offered to the other provinces. Even though it meant
introducing into the process of Senate reform an additional and useless
rigidity. The Senate is the principal target for constitutional reform of a
West thwarted by the provincialism of Canada's political system.

In this same Meech Lake Accord, limitations on federal spending power, originally requested by Quebec to protect its jurisdictions,
were applied to all provinces. Once again, because of the effect of the
Conquest, we were careful not to take into account that national spending
programs in areas of provincial competence were accepted much better
in English Canada than in Quebec. Not surprisingly, the move worried
the small provinces that depend very much on federal programs. And
those who oppose the Meech Lake Accord have maintained that these
provisions would alarmingly decrease the ability of the federal government to act, in the context of free trade with the United States.

This is clear evidence of the deeply vicious side of a dynamic
based on the denial of the political consequences of Quebec's specificity.
The Meech Lake Accord has been accused of weakening Canada and
impeding the just expectations of the West. No one wanted to see that,
on the contrary, it was the refusal to openly recognize Quebec's specificity that gave Prince Edward Island the right to veto Senate reform or that

complicated Ottawa's exercise of spending power in areas agreed upon by all of English Canada. If the Meech Lake Accord were to be modified in order to correct these deficiencies, it should be to more completely recognize Quebec's specificity.

For Quebec within Canada can only have a particular status, in fact if not in law. This evidence has become the taboo *par excellence* in Canadian politics; simply pronouncing the words "unique status" (which smell of regressive favouritism) would be suicide for any English-Canadian politician. This says a great deal about the Canadian problem.

Increased provincialism serves no one. Who would dare say that the country is "just fine" when, in 1982, the Constitution was repatriated and amended in spite of Quebec's disagreement, whereas, six years later, Manitoba alone was able to block the Meech Lake Accord?

THE TORONTO-OTTAWA-MONTREAL AXIS

I've claimed in this book that Canada was built on the Conquest of 1760. But we mustn't forget that, for the past century, the country has also been built largely on the exploitation of its peripheral regions, the Atlantic and the West. Quebecers are often not enough aware of this reality.

Prime Minister Sir John A. Macdonald's "National Policy" of the last century laid the foundations of modern Canada. Through increased taxes on imported American goods and the game of rail tariffs, the West became a reservoir of raw materials for Quebec and Ontario, as well as a captive market for products manufactured in those two populated and industrialized provinces. That was the country's original reality; it was not, as such, prejudiced against the interests of the peripheral regions. But the situation still evolved to their disadvantage.

The Atlantic provinces were reduced to a state of chronic dependency on the federal government, from which it is difficult for them to break away today because, among other reasons, they are partly resigned to their fate. The situation in the West is not the same. This younger, wealthier region is frustrated in feeling itself economically exploited by a federal power that favours Central Canada. The recently defunct national policy on energy was interpreted in the West as an enormous and unjustified transfer of the resources of oil-producing provinces to the consumers in the East.

Because the West resented being colonized by Central Canada, it often used the most obvious component of that part of the country,

French Quebec, as its scapegoat. It was easier to blame people who were different, in a fundamental element such as language, than to blame anonymous bankers, good family men of Bay Street and St. James Street. This feeling could be understood as long as the Toronto-Ottawa-Montreal axis controlled the country and as long as Quebec was an integral part of Central Canada.

Well, this is no longer the case in many respects; and everything indicates that it will be less and less so. In the manner of the West, Quebec has become a region, but a French region. The rise of Quebec nationalism and the province's francisization have pushed the core of the old Anglo-Montreal power to flee to Toronto. That movement is not unrelated to the Ontario capital's economic expansion over the past few years. Its highest building proudly displays the name of the Bank of Montreal, whose head office in Montreal today is only symbolic.

The luxurious era of the entrepreneurs of Montreal's Golden Square Mile[4] is long gone. During the second half of the nineteenth century, they laid the foundation, thanks to the railway, of Canada's economic empire. During that period, the Anglo-Montreal Establishment looked down from its towers on provincial Toronto; all that is left are a few sumptuous souvenirs. The majestic Sun Life building, at one time the highest in the Commonwealth, still dominates Dominion Square. To Quebec nationalism, it has come to symbolize Anglo-Saxon arrogance.

Central Canada is becoming more and more restricted to Ontario, where an unequaled percentage of Canada's population and wealth are concentrated. Quebec will probably have the same kind of complaints about this new central Canada as the West has. The Quebec Premier's criticisms of a federal monetary policy based on a Torontonian economic situation that is harmful to the rest of the country are precursory signs of his province's more regional and economic alienation.

But, for as long as the specific aspects of Quebec nationalism are not recognized, Quebec's regional energy will not be able to work in concert with the West. And the West will be angry with Quebec for imposing on it priorities that are often those of Ontario and for projecting the image of a power that has moved elsewhere—all in the name of bilingualism.

A partial solution to regional alienation could come with the reform of federal institutions, especially the Senate. It would be necessary to ensure that, in their formulation, federal policies took more into consideration the concerns of the country's various regions. Senate reform has always been "the" constitutional demand of the West.

Quebec's traditional position has been not to get involved in Senate reform, whose success would have weakened the province's principal constitutional claim: a modification of the division of powers between Ottawa and Quebec. This non-interest, combined with the fact that a real Senate reform would considerably modify Canadian politics, has made the prospect of such a change illusory until now.

Recognition of Quebec's specificity, on the condition that it does have political effects, would change this way of seeing things. Recognition would separate Quebec's special responsibility in regard to the province's distinct society from the province's concerns as a region within the country. The Government of Quebec would then have an interest in using its power of veto over federal insititutions, not to block any reform of the Senate, but to ensure that eventual changes would reflect its new interests as a region.

Quebec and the West's global support of free trade was a good indication of the new convergence of interests between these two regions. That reality was in sharp contrast to the opposition of an isolated Ontario Government, which expressed its solemn rejection in a resolution of the province's Legislative Assembly. It should not be deduced that, from now on, the combined forces of Quebec and the West will allow them to govern Canada against the wishes of the powerful province that (although this wasn't too obvious) was the principal benefactor of the constitutional changes of 1982.

In many areas, the interests of what used to be Upper and Lower Canada still blend. And one must not underestimate the consequences of the physical distance between Quebec and the West or downplay the anti-French tradition in the latter region. Within the country, too, there is a uniquely English-Canadian solidarity against Quebec. And, we must remember, provincialism has clearly become more important than regionalism. The West, like Quebec, globally supported free trade, but it is also in this region, in Saskatchewan, that the Canadian-American treaty met with the most opposition during the election campaign of 1988.

Even with these reservations, it is unprecedented that an agreement as important as free trade was concluded in spite of Ontario's opposition. In other ways, it is clear that the magnitude of Toronto's growth is a sign of the upsetting of the balance of Canada's geopolitical system. Ontario's colossus has feet of clay. Alone, it will never generate as much power as the old Toronto-Ottawa-Montreal axis.

The Free Trade Agreement with the United States, in stimulating Canada's latent regionalism, should weaken Ontario's hegemony over the country by transforming the province more into a region like the others...undoubtedly a strong region—as the Ontario business world's massive support of the Accord has proven. Some English Canadians, not all of whom live in Ontario, fear that the agreement will cause a dangerous "Balkanization" of the country and that the Federal Government's powers will be weakened disproportionately.

But we are forgetting that the process, within the Canadian reality, will not be able to go beyond certain limits. It is difficult to see how the Atlantic provinces could forego federal aid; and most of the reforms of the Trudeau era, which leaned toward the reinforcement of central power, would stay. But a rise in regionalism would be both a breath of fresh air and a return to the source of Canada's original strength. It would also alleviate the most pernicious consequences of the reforms of 1982.

This would finally enable Quebec's own regional dynamism to express itself inside Canada...on the condition, of course, that Quebec's specificity be recognized. The Free Trade Agreement, far from rendering this recognition perilous or obsolete, increases its necessity. The country has no other choice but to better integrate Quebec nationalist energy and the dynamism of its regions, if it wants to be able to accept the challenge of a difficult rendezvous with the American giant.

In this light, the constitutional reforms of 1982, the Free Trade Agreement with the United States, and the recognition of the political consequences of Quebec's specificity must be considered as a whole. These three measures supplement and complement one another. Separately, they can destroy the country. Together, they will change the country as much as the British North America Act of 1867 changed the destiny of these disparate colonies in the north of the continent, which England didn't really know what to do with.

One question remains: Is Canada still capable of change?

CHAPTER 9

What is English Canada?

Some English Canadians are surprised that we still speak to them about an "English Canada" and about those Americans who refused independence in order to remain faithful to the King of England:

"Toronto has become a multicultural metropolis, the largest French-language city in Canada outside Quebec. Saskatchewan is about to become bilingual. And the other provinces all differ from each other. Ontario is more like Quebec than Newfoundland.

Long live Canada! Its bilingualism, its mosaic, its ... "

*

What if English Canada still existed? And what if this were Canada's last chance?

CANADIAN IDEALISM

Idealism. That is the after-effect of the Conquest that is specifically Canadian, one the country would hold onto even if Quebec were to leave.

The Conquest was originally Quebec's problem. But, over the two hundred years from Briand, to Laurier, to Riel and all the way to Trudeau, it has become Canada's problem...because of what was, or rather what was not, English Canada. After the structural reforms of French Power, the phenomenon now affects, to varying degrees, the entire system. Bilingualism, Multiculturalism, the Charter of Rights, Provincialism. We've already mentioned the harmful effects of the ideal of provincial equality, if taken too far.

It is not that the reforms were not necessary. To the contrary. They correspond to the reality of a country that has two languages, numerous ethnic groups, strong provinces, and citizens respectful of human rights. Whether they all share in the ideal does not present any difficulties either. All countries, all national identities, need a minimum of official mythology to survive. You only have to look at nations such as France, England, and the United States to see that.

But, beyond the reality of the country, beyond the ideal, Canada is foundering in an idealism, in the ideology of the ideal, that is constraining and compulsory. That is not surprising: in politics, idealism corresponds to losing touch with reality. It results from an inability to integrate some aspects of that reality. It is well known that the principal artisan of French Power, Pierre Elliot Trudeau, based the main part of his actions on the negation of the political consequences generated naturally by the Quebec Fact. Reality is simply taking its revenge.

The official line on multiculturalism implies that assimilation of an ethnic group in Canada is not inevitable. In the ideal of the mosaic there is a desire to avoid the Quebec phenomenon, as well as any expression of those undeniably Canadian qualities: tolerance and the spirit of compromise. This is a partially successful attempt to exorcise the essence of Canada's identity problem: its difficulty with affirming values that are its own.

But, idealism somewhat spoils the sauce. Some Ottawa multi-cultural theorists seriously claim that Canada's characteristic is not only that it is open to all cultures, but that it does not favour any, not even its own. A Canadian of East Indian origin, a member of the Royal Canadian Mounted Police, has had recognized his right to wear a turban on duty. Even the "Mounties," one of the principal symbols of a Canadian mythology that is oddly lacking in them, do not carry more weight than the multicultural ideal.

That is only a minor point. The problem becomes more serious when idealisms mount up: bilingualism and the Charter of Rights, in the case of immersion classes for example. In a country where one quarter of the population is Francophone, one can only applaud the phenomenon of French-immersion classes for Anglophones. This demonstrates an evident opening of English Canada's mind toward the Francophone and Québécois reality.

Bilingualism has become, as well, a major component of the official Canadian identity. An eloquent symbol. Anyone now aspiring to be Prime Minister must be able to speak French[1]. Consequently, ambitious English Canadians are taking steps to ensure their children learn French and thus have the possibility of national careers.

In English Canada, the popularity of immersion classes is so great that, in most places, there are more Anglophones wanting to learn French than there are Francophones in total. However, the latter insist, and rightly so, on having schools where the majority of students have French as their first language, with all that implies politically and culturally: the use of French outside class; control of the administration, and so on.

This seems like a simple matter of common sense. But some people claim that the request would be unconstitutional, that you couldn't make a distinction between Francophones who wanted to study in their own language and Anglophones who wanted to learn French as a second language. That would be language discrimination…prohibited by the Canadian Charter of Rights.

This reasoning is perfectly understandable in a system that is trying its utmost to dissociate language from identity. If we are not careful, this system's idealism will turn against the francophone minorities we originally wanted to protect. In English Canada, French-language schools will become immersion schools, where French will be learned as a second language. Many Francophones, already bilingual, would doubtless prefer French schools in which Anglophones are a majority, rather than no French schools at all.

Praise the Lord! In Canada there are a lot of people with common sense who, up to now, have toned down the most absurd effects of the country's official idealism. The damage is still limited, but the dynamic is encrusted in the constitutional framework of Canada and has only begun to take effect. It is now weakening relationships between Quebec and the rest of the country, relationships between Francophones and Anglophones.

Over the past few years, we have witnessed sporadic manifestations of English Canada's frustrations with Quebec, the "spoiled child that never stops complaining." As usual, these feelings are particularly evident in the Prairies. Manitoba has taken to heart the fact that Ottawa granted to a Quebec aeronautic firm a contract to maintain CF-18 military aircraft.

These feelings surfaced in the West during the federal election campaign in the autumn of 1988, leading to the election of some Liberal MPs. They grew visibly stronger in December 1988, in the wake of Quebec's decision to remove itself from the Supreme Court's decision on Bill 101's provision concerning the language of signs. The government of Manitoba cited this action as its reason for withdrawing its support of the Meech Lake Accord.

If regional rivalries are normal in a federal regime, it is still revealing to note that, in the Prairies, Quebec remains the favourite target, while Ontario continues to profit more practically from federalism. And, despite the high visibility of the CF-18s, the French province is generally not treated any better than the three central provinces. These past few years, the Federal Government has invested a great deal of money in helping the farmers in this region of the country who are in difficulty. At great cost, it saved some of their financial institutions from bankruptcy.

Is this a modern version of the old English-French antagonism? Certainly. But, why especially in the Prairies? Why now? The increased irritability toward Quebec followed a debate, which received a great deal of media attention during the spring and summer of 1988, on the imposition of bilingualism in Saskatchewan and Alberta. The strongest opposition to the recognition of Quebec as a distinct society comes from

Manitoba (the West's formally bilingual province), from political fig-
ures but also from local communities.

It is difficult not to relate these reactions to the Canadian judicial
system's discovery in 1979 (just before the Quebec Referendum) of the
fact that this massively anglophone province had never legally ceased to
be bilingual. The Canadian political Establishment had then unanimously applauded this "late but much-merited victory of bilingualism."
They pretended to forget that the majority of the Manitoba population
clearly did not share their enthusiasm.

The West is now Anglophone. Canadian duality has been
merely symbolic there since the Riel defeat. The historic settlement of
Francophones in this region of the country, and the presence of Quebec
in the Canadian federation, make bilingualism there indispensable at the
federal level. But that cannot make us forget that the Canadian duality,
in the reality to the west of Ontario, no longer has enough basis to justify
bilingualism on the provincial level.

It is not surprising, then, that such an extension of bilingualism
to the provincial level is considered by many as a futile attempt to rewrite
history, and an unprovoked aggression by Quebec. From a Western point
of view, Quebec is unilingually French and wants to be recognized as a
distinct society...while at the same time exercising an influence in
Ottawa that they can only dream of in Winnipeg.

Human nature being what it is, the nuances quickly fall by the
wayside. Provincial bilingualism turns into federal bilingualism. Necessary measures, such as the federal law on official languages and then the
recognition of Quebec's specificity, are being questioned once again—
not only in the Prairies, but in all of English Canada.

This is the vicious circle that intensifies tension between Quebec
and the West, two regions that have never before had so much in
common. It also increases the level of animosity between English
Canada in general and Quebec. In this context, there is unfortunately no
assurance (as some would like us to believe) that some of these ferociously anti-Quebec reactions emanate from dinosaurs doomed to extinction.

Is it really desirable that a 97 percent anglophone province such
as Saskatchewan become bilingual? Should the serious politicians of
that province be reduced to making promises that the next generation will
be French-speaking? Is it not disquieting that we can no longer see—that
we don't want to see—that a massively anglophone province far away
from Quebec cannot become bilingual beyond certain limits? And what
about the other side of the coin...the fact that the majority of the Quebec

population would feel institutional bilingualism at the provincial level as an aggressive action of the first order?

It will be difficult to tone down the Canadian idealism, even slightly. That would force Canadians and Quebecers to confront the discomforting realities that they have so carefully avoided until today.

AN ENGLISH CANADA IN HIDING

English Canada? It's the sophisticated torpor of Victoria and the Saskatchewan farmers who fear that free trade will dismantle the Canadian Wheat Commission. The Newfoundlanders feel insular and exploited by Quebec on hydro-electricity. You'll find English Canada in multicultural Toronto, where the old anglo-protestant work ethic reigns more strongly than ever.

English Canada? It is also all the elites that wanted to learn French, often with enthusiasm. Without a doubt, bilingualism did change the country. The Canadian ideal—Trudeau/Mulroney—not only speaks in two languages, it lives fully in the two cultures. Within the Canadian elites, bilingualism is no longer reserved for Francophones, as it used to be. More and more, it is a requisite for admission to the country's governing circles. Clearly, there is a future for this influential minority, within a Canada that needs to build a bridge between Franco-phones and Anglophones. Right away, this is a fine Québécois victory.

It did not take much for some to forget that a bridge is only important in relation to the two banks of the river that it joins. In time, and with the help of the effect of the Conquest, the structure came to replace the principle. English Canada no longer exists; the Quebec distinct society is passé. Only Canada remains, where Canadians speak English or French, and soon English and French. Some forget that it wasn't bil-ingualism that made the country, that it cannot ensure its survival, and that it could even lead to its destruction.

At certain crucial moments, English Canadians have been Quebecers' best allies: from the Loyalists who joined the Anciens Canadiens in the 1770s, to Robert Baldwin's reformists who allied themselves with Louis-Hippolyte LaFontaine in the 1840s to mend the mess of the Union. And on to the unilingual, obstinate Anglophones who, in 1981, insisted that the new Canadian Charter of Rights and Freedoms include the "notwithstanding" clause.

English Canada still exists, but it feels fragile; weakened, it tends to vacillate. We saw this during the 1988 election campaign, when the country shouted, before a bewildered Quebec, its visceral fear of free trade with the United States. The usual manifestation of English Canada's difficulty in existing is its refusal to flaunt itself. This is the exact opposite of the Quebec identity's exaggerated dependency on image. The one balances the other, and this is not accidental. A two hundred year-old cohabitation does leave its marks.

By definition, the English-Canadian identity is anti-American. No wonder a highly Americanized English-Canadian society no longer recognizes its right to exist alone and to step out from under its cosmetic facade of bilingualism and multiculturalism. If the Quebecers as a collectivity have remained at the Conquest of 1760, English Canada has never recovered from the defeat of the Loyalists, at the hands of the Americans, only fifteen years later. English Canada relives this defeat each day of its life.

In anglophone nationalist circles there is a growing fear, then, of the political consequences of a growing liberalization of trade with the United States. The transformation of the 1988 electoral campaign into an emotion-filled referendum on the subject only confused those who had forgotten that the national phenomenon is, largely, psychological. It was obviously not enough to convince the English Canadians of the economic benefits of Free Trade. And it was not only because they believed in the positive spin-offs that Francophones reacted differently to the gamble.

English-Canadian nationalists now feel, in regard to the survival of their identity, a fear very much like that of Quebec nationalists. Quebecers dread being assimilated by the Anglophones: Anglophones do not want to become Americans. Both are terrified of disappearing. Until now, the intensity of this double agony has rendered them incapable of recognizing to what extent they need each other to survive. That has always been Canada's tragedy. Because of the sequels of the Conquest, the union has not come about, or has come about poorly.

So Quebec nationalism remained immovable in its support of Free Trade, without realizing that the English-Canadian nationalists' fear of being Americanized was the same as its own fears, that a slip in the agreement with the United States would, in a way, turn Quebecers into Franco-Americans. During this time, English Canada, by pulling back on its support of the Meech Lake Accord, is sawing away at the very branch on which it is sitting, unaware that the Quebec identity is really pushed to its limit. The haunting fear of extinction grows within each group. The incompatibility grows between their will to live and their ability to recognize one another, as different, one within the other: Quebec within Canada; the English Fact in the Quebec society.

Canada has always suffered from an identity problem, which many attributed to its binational character. "We should build a real country, establish a real Canadian nation." But Canada is not a normal country, and probably never will be. That, as they say, is its fate. Far from having been its weakness, its binational characteristic has always been its real strength.

By working to become "normal countries," each at the other's expense, Canada and Quebec are destroying themselves. What is eating away at both of them, leading Anglophones to new heights of Americanization and Francophones to increased assimilation, is their inability to get over the Conquest. That is one reason why the twentieth century, despite the hopes of Laurier, will definitely not have been the "century of Canada."

It is becoming more and more apparent that the ideas of the leader of French Power, insofar as they were meant to prolong the effect of the Conquest, were quite successful with a new generation of English-Canadian politicians. The most adamant opponents of the recognition of the political effects of Quebec's specificity are often young and bilingual. They present themselves as defenders of Francophones outside Quebec, of the Anglo-Quebecers, women, ethnic groups, and of all those Canadians "who should not become second-class citizens."

These disciples of Pierre Elliot Trudeau are not opposed, or so they say, to the recognition of Quebec as a distinct society. They simply want to improve upon the Meech Lake Accord. They are asking governments not only to protect but to promote their linguistic minorities; they are insisting that the Canadian Charter of Rights take precedence over the distinct society clause. Who could be against human rights or minority rights?

The man who inspired them obviously gives the sense of these statements: Quebec's specificity must not have political consequences. Well, it would be in Canada's self-interest that it did, even if it were not a question of justice, a question of honour, in regard to a Quebec that trusted the rest of the country in 1980.

To what extent does English Canada still exist? The fact that the simple recognition of Quebec as a distinct society takes on for some the aspect of a traumatic mini-separation says much about English Canada's difficulty to confront, alone, the reality of its Americanization. During the 1960s, English Canadians often asked the question of Quebecers: "What does Quebec want?" Slightly modified, the question should be thrown back: "What is English Canada?"

CHAPTER 10

The Quebec Challenge

The novelty of the Meech Lake Accord was the breach it opened in the principal effect of the conquest. It was recognized that Quebec constituted a distinct society, and that that had political effects. The Government of Quebec had only the duty to protect Canadian duality on its territory, while it must not only protect but also promote the distinct Quebec society at home. Politically, everything was there.

The day after the signing of the Accord, a caricature in the *Toronto Star* depicted a Canadian flag with nine maple leaves and a fleur-de-lis in the middle. The picture was worth a thousand words: recognition was minimal, but it was there. Trudeau was not mistaken, and his criticisms would not end until the Accord was dead and buried. As for everything else, in the image of Canada, the agreement was superbly imperfect and ambiguous—the first manifestation in a long time of that pragmatic spirit of compromise that had always been the basis of Canada in everything operational.

Although highly criticized, the judicialization of the system would probably have benefited Quebec society, allowing it to avoid immediately defining what it would become later. At present, such a definition would sacrifice too much of Quebec's specificity on the altar of the French image; to the very great danger of the French language itself. Judges are neither extraterrestrials nor pure spirits; the interpretations of a constitutional text must be subject to the influence of an evolving reality. In this sense, the Meech Lake Accord would have been what Quebecers and Canadians made of it.

A good example of this phenomenon occurred in December, 1988, when the Supreme Court passed judgment on Bill 101. It was decided then that Quebec could impose a marked predominance of French, on the condition that another language not be prohibited. Few realized that this judgment corresponded to the spirit of the Meech Lake Accord, which was not even part of the Canadian Constitution.

The judges were obviously influenced by the current debates and consensuses that seemed to be coming out on the political level. They took it for granted that the Meech Lake Accord would be ratified and that common sense and respect for one's word would prevail. As soon as this prospect began to fade, what choice would they have but to interpret the Constitution as it had been rewritten by Trudeau in 1982—on the basis of individual rights and institutional bilingualism from one ocean to the other? Judgments will at times be contradictory, but that is where we are heading, in the spirit of a system that is voluntarily incompatible with the specificity of the Quebec society and that holds constitutional precedence over it.

In Quebec, systematically placing the two languages on the same footing is something fundamentally different from the possibility for the English reality to show itself within a French society. Seen solely from the viewpoint of individual rights, Quebec's simple imposition of French predominance is discriminatory, for it implies that the Francophone is superior to the Anglophone.

Fortunately, there is the "notwithstanding" clause, also part of the Constitution. The Supreme Court decision concerning signs facilitated the use of this clause, to the benefit of everyone. And it allowed us to avoid the worst: a head-on collision between the French Quebec of Bill 101 and the bilingual Canada of French Power. There was a great crash, and a few broken spars and debris, as when two great ships pass too closely in the night.

Quebecers and Canadians owe acknowledgement to the Anglo-Saxon common sense of those Western premiers who, in 1981, insisted on the inclusion of this "imperfection" in the beautiful Canadian Charter of Rights. The old British tradition—the old Quebec tradition—of parliamentary sovereignty wasn't so bad. For the resentment of many English Canadians following Quebec's use of the "notwithstanding" clause is nothing compared to what would have been triggered in Quebec, in December 1988, with the official end of an exclusively French face.

In theory, the "notwithstanding" clause grants Quebec tremendous power, enabling it to elude the essential aspects of the Constitutional Charter of Rights. If the rest of the country were to agree to abolish the provision, some believe it would be possible for Quebec to keep the clause for itself alone[1]. Paradoxically, the Supreme Court decision, which most Quebecers saw as something to mourn, was perhaps their greatest victory since the Referendum: the powers of the only government they controlled were consolidated. Above all, their Premier Robert Bourassa was strong enough to use immediately the "notwithstanding" clause in the name of the collectivity he represented.

The derogation clause enables Quebec to maintain its exclusively French face, which the Meech Lake Accord alone would probably not have permitted, even admitting that it had political consequences. It is tempting for Quebecers not to mourn for long the anticipated failure of the agreement. Do they not have the possibility of paralyzing the system on the constitutional level? Did they not recover the veto…by the back door?

Quebec will forget at its own risk that it cannot prevent the ten other Canadian governments from changing the rules of the game when they really want to. A spectacular demonstration of this came in 1982 when they patriated and modified the Constitution without the approval of the Quebec government, while inserting the "notwithstanding" clause that Quebec is now taking advantage of. But above all, Quebec is still vulnerable because it has often demonstrated its difficulty in exercising its power under the disapproving eye of the "English." And now, the "notwithstanding" clause can only be implemented under the more and more disapproving eye of the rest of the country and of a part of the Quebec identity itself. If the past is hostage to the future, the "notwithstanding" clause will probably turn against a Quebec that uses it too often. A boomerang clause…

It is still an indispensable insurance policy, to be kept as a just-in-case dissuasive and defensive tool. However, only the recognition by the rest of Canada of the political effects of Quebec's specificity will allow the Quebec society to truly blossom, instead of being reduced to defending itself, in an ever more inefficient and regressive manner. Independence itself would require recognition of the geopolitical environment of North America.

This recognition faces tremendous obstacles, even in a minimal version such as the Meech Lake Accord. Whoever knows Quebec at all, knows that it is impossible for it to go any further. If the foreseeable result becomes a reality, if the Meech Lake Accord is rejected, the impasse will be complete; a political solution will no longer be possible. Ratification of the Accord today would not have the same impact as it would have a year ago. A rolling stone gathers no moss, but the agreement has not been rolling.

A constitution is more than a legal text of Sibylline articles over which pompous experts ponder. A constitution is a combination of symbols, values, and emotions that "make" a country. In Canada, it doesn't seem that the Quebec society is part of that combination. The answer will be made officially known June 23, 1990, the Eve of Saint-Jean-Baptiste Day ...

It is impossible to resolve a problem that cannot be seen. At the very least, the endless agony of the Meech Lake Accord could serve to illuminate the true problem and its gravity—a stunning display of a country's dependence on the Conquest. And what if the problem proved to be more and more difficult to get round or resolve? Why not take a moment to look towards the end of the cul de sac? Who knows what may come of it?

It would be most deceptive to underestimate the need of many persons to just not see. A growing number of Quebecers are once again dreaming of independence. Most English Canadians are betting on the quiet standardization of "la Belle Province." Some of them, among the most favourable, now maintain that there will be no delay in ratifying the Accord, which would deprive the country of the benefit of at least an openly recognized failure.

Life goes on. In Canada and Quebec, people are quite used to this type of crisis. We have so often cried "Wolf!" without anything very serious happening after all. The great majority of Canadians and Quebecers believe that all of this, at the bottom, isn't so tragic and, in any case, the country will always be protected from a bad skid.

A dangerous illusion! There are many dormant elements of a disaster from which no country or society is *a priori* exempt. History can prove tragic for anyone. The brief FLQ interlude was without a follow-up because of Trudeau's vigorous reaction, but also because the Parti Québécois coming into being was able to channel the energies and frustrations of the apprentice-terrorists. Beyond the Meech Lake Accord, however, there is no political solution in sight.

The rest of the country will have to accept responsibility for its rejection of Meech Lake. It would be too easy for Quebecers to wash their hands of the affair, to forget that, if Quebec cannot get itself recognized as a distinct society, it is also because most Quebec nationalists only paid lip service, if they did anything, to the Accord. The tremendous energy of Quebec nationalism was hardly brought to bear in support of the agreement; some messages were not sent to the rest of the country when they should have been. Many aspired to an entirely French and, if possible, independent society rather than to a distinct society within Canada.

Some of the most respected members of the intelligentsia have devalued, even ridiculed, Quebec's undeniable success in intergovernmental relations within Canada: "To be reduced to a distinct society…" They were perturbed that, to control Ottawa's spending power in provincial fields of competence, it would be necessary to cite a power that had been in use for sixty years. Beneath the technical or juridical objections, the Accord's greatest flaw for many was that it implied a recognition of Canada. It is not surprising that the agreement's expected failure does not displease everybody. Quebec hasn't signed anything; it doesn't recognize the Constitution; it isn't really part of Canada. The future is saved.

During that future, the Federal Government's power to spend can continue to be exercised, without control, in fields of competence exclusive to Quebec. The integration of Quebec society into Canada increases every day in innumerable areas of daily life, and on the basis of the negation of the political consequences of Quebec's specificity. And during that future, the solemn rejection of Quebec has no legal effect on a Canadian Constitution still integrally applicable to that province, including the "notwithstanding" clause.

During that future, finally, no one is trying to exorcise some of the demons that have been haunting Quebec for more than two centuries and that mortgage its future, whatever that future may be. No one is trying to integrate the fact that there was a Conquest—which cannot be reversed—so that the Conquest will stop producing new and perverse effects and so that Jean Chrétien will not become both Prime Minister and *John Chretien*. No one is mourning a Quebec that could have been, so that the Quebec that exists can now take wing.

How can the fear of disappearing, which is at the heart of Quebec's identity, be transformed into an advantage? How can one think a little about "the unthinkable"? Answers to these questions would enable the Quebec people to better evaluate the true dangers of assimilation and, especially, of "folklorization." They would know when the strength of image is deteriorating into an image of strength. And, in general, they would better manage Quebec's power.

Not without reason, francophone Quebecers are worried about their collective future. They have learned a great deal since 1960, however. They have been faced with so many new elements and have fought in the midst of so many contradictions that many of them are now looking forward to a synthesis. They know well that there is no miracle recipe and that they will not relive 1970, 1976, or 1980. But, beyond the dreams, ideologies, and dogmas, the Quebec people can show a clear appreciation of their geopolitical situation and of what is at stake because of it. What they care most about is being able to live in French and witness the end of a certain kind of Anglo-Saxon arrogance toward them. As for the rest, beneath the surrounding pessimism, Quebec society may be more ready than we think to elaborate a new consensus and once again to have children.

Some will say that it would be naive, even masochistic, for Quebec to tear itself apart by recognizing its Canadian component, while the other side of the problem still exists and the rest of the country stubbornly refuses to admit the natural political consequences of Quebec's specificity. This is, undeniably, a strong argument for staying with the *status quo* while waiting for English Canada to listen to reason or until Independence comes.

Some may argue that Canada's problem does not excuse Quebec from confronting its own, and that, on the contrary, Quebec would emerge the stronger from this difficult exercise, in a position to impose upon the rest of Canada a fundamentally different relationship. Such an independent step would not necessarily lead to formal independence, but it would be more advantageous for the future than the naive wishes that people use to camouflage their helplessness.

The challenge would be great...but so is Quebec.

In the wake of the failure of the Meech Lake Accord it would be a grave error for Quebec to abandon the concept of a distinct society, intrinsically French, with an English component. Used, developed, enriched, this concept should prove fruitful on many levels and to unsuspected degrees. Its great strength is, paradoxically, its minimal character and its adherence to the reality of contemporary Quebec, while remaining dynamic and open to the future.

By comparison, the rigid, official Canada that has come out of the past quarter century seems older than its years... too backward in relation to the reality of the country to be able to guarantee its survival.

POSTSCRIPT TO THE ENGLISH EDITION

One year after the publication of *Le défi québécois*, political events in this country have more than confirmed, I think, the main thesis of the essay.

It is clear now, more then ever, that the relationship between Quebec and the rest of the country doesn't work anymore. Whatever the fate of the Meech Lake Accord, that relationship should be fundamentally changed. English Canadians should be aware that the real crisis still lies ahead, probably after a latent phase following the Meech Lake Accord debate. The writing is on the wall: The Canadian and the Quebecois identities have become too entangled for their respective good, and there is a deep antagonistic dynamic between them, as this book has tried to show.

To alleviate the most dangerous aspects of this situation, we must find ways to ensure that Quebec and the rest of the country take some distance. At the very least, a form of psychological separation would be good for everybody. We must remember too that a crisis is also an opportunity to build a better future for us all.

Quebec will have to confront problems of its own. As for English Canada, is it able to renounce the privileges of the Conquest of 1763, on which this country is still structurally built? Is Canada capable of frankly accepting that Quebec is not only a province unlike the others, but that Quebec's difference has real political consequences? I hope so. Because if the answer to these questions is no, there is no doubt in my mind that more and more Quebecers will choose the difficult but stimulating task of building a country of their own, after which they have yearned for so long.

During the Meech Lake Debate, many English Canadians expressed feelings of love to Quebecers, sometimes in moving ways. This kindness touched them. But that shouldn't make anyone forget that what Quebec really needs from the rest of the country is more respect than love.

Christian Dufour
Quebec City, June 1990

CHRONOLOGY 1759-1791

-Summer 1759: English torch the parishes of the Quebec region.

-September 1759: Battle of the Plains of Abraham; Surrender of Quebec.

-October 1759-June 1760: France suspends payment of paper money.

-May 8, 1760: Death of the last Bishop of the French Regime, Mgr. de Pontbriand.

-August 21, 1760: Brigadier James Murray torches Sorel and surrounding areas.

-September 8, 1760: Surrender of Montreal and New France, Freedom of religion granted. Beginning of martial law; Murray is military governor of Quebec.

-February 4, 1762: *Te Deum* played in Canadien churches in honour of the King of England, George III.

-1762: a gift of 20 £ from Murray to Briand.

-November 22, 1762: End of the Seven Years War.

-February 10, 1763: Treaty of Paris gives Canada to England (Article 4 no longer guarantees the freedom of religion).

-September 15, 1763: Attempt to elect Mgr. Montgolfier as head of the Canadien Church. Murray vetoes.

-October 7, 1763: Royal Proclamation denies Canadiens' civil, political, and religious rights.

-1763-1764: Insurrection of Indian Chief Pontiac.

-August 10, 1764: Effective date of the Royal Proclamation; Murray is first civil governor; end of martial law. Beginning of the French Party.

-September 11, 1764: Ecclesiastic chapter of Quebec elects Briand as head of the Canadien Church.

-Autumn 1764-autumn 1765: Briand visits London.

-September 1764: Murray reorganizes the administration of justice, setting aside part of the Royal Proclamation.

-October 1764: Canadiens petition against the Royal Proclamation.

-1764: First publication of the *Quebec Gazette* (bilingual).

-June 10, 1765: Anti-Catholic provisions of the English Penal Code are declared nonapplicable to Canadiens.

-January 21, 1766: Pontifical bull authorizes the nomination of a Quebec bishop.

-March 16, 1766: Briand consecrated Bishop in France.

-June 28, 1766: Briand returns to Quebec City as Bishop.

-Summer 1766: Carleton is second governor of Canada.

-1772: Mgr. Briand's circular prohibits aid to deserters.

-1774: Quebec Act recognizes French civil law and Catholicism; broadens the borders of the Province of Quebec.

-October 21, 1774: American colony protests the Quebec Act.

-May 1, 1775: Effective date of the Act of Quebec.

-1775-1776: First American invasion of Canada: first Loyalist arrivals; birth of English Canada.

-June 1778: Departure of Carleton; arrival of the third governor of Canada, Haldimand.

-1780: Briand named adjutor-Bishop.

-1784: Irish Catholics acquire their first right to land possession.

-1786: Carleton returns as governor, for the second time, under the name Lord Dorchester. Briand is no longer Bishop. End of the French Party.

-July 14, 1789: Beginning of the French Revolution.

-June 10, 1791: Constitutional Act instituting an Elective Assembly and creating Upper and Lower Canada; beginnings of the Canadian Nation.

NOTES

INTRODUCTION

1. In this book, the expression "provincialism" refers to the notion that everything that is Canada's fundamental political entity is the province, all provinces being equal in status.

CHAPTER 1

1. Wolfe's Proclamation, June 27, 1759, as quoted by Michel Brunet in *La présence anglaise et les Canadiens,* Beauchemin, Montreal, 1958.
2. *Id.*, p. 42.
3. Quoted by Lionel Groulx, *Lendemains de Conquéte*, Stanké, coll. "10 X 10", Montreal, 1977, p. 127-128.
4. Quoted by Mason Wade in *The French Canadians, 1760-1968,* vol. 1, MacMillan, Toronto, 1968, p. 48.
5. Quoted by Mason Wade, *ibid*, p. 56.
6. During that time, the population of France was 20 million. There were only 65,000 inhabitants in New France. The population of England was 8 million. There were 1,500,000 inhabitants in the American Colonies.
7. Marjorie G. Reid, "Pitt's decision to keep Canada in 1761", in Cameron Nish, *The French Canadians 1759-1766*, Copp Clark Publishing Company, Montreal, 1966. One of the reasons the English Prime Minister would have decided to keep Canada would have been nothing less than France's offer to give it up. Paris preferred Guadeloupe to New France.
8. Under the very militarized regime of New France, the Canadiens had an exceptional military reputation that terrified the Bostonians.
9. Kenneth D. McRae, "The structure of Canadian History", quoted by Louis Hartz in *The Founding of New Societies,* New York, 1964, Chapter 7, p. 231.
10. Quoted in Cameron Nish, *The French Canadians 1759-1766. Conquered? Half-Conquered? Liberated?* Copp Clark Publishing Company, Montreal, 1966, p. 75.
11. *Id.*, p. 121. *Id.*, p. 86.
12. This brings to mind at least two leaders of the Canadian Party in the early 19th century: Papineau and Nelson.
13. Public Archives of Canada. Documents concerning the Constitution of Canada, vol. 1, *Capitulation of Montréal*, art. 27 and 30.
14. Public Archives of Canada, "Documents concerning the Constitution of Canada, vol.

15. There is a famous quarrel amongst Quebec historians (Hamelin/Ouellet/Nish/ Brunet/Fregault) on the following point: in 1760, in New France, was there a commercial bourgeoisie class ruined by the Conquest whose supplies and contact with France were cut off? The main point that concerns us is the fact that, after 1763, there is no doubt that there was not a strong bourgeoisie class in Canada.

16. Quoted by Hilda Neatby, "Jean Olivier Briand, a minor Canadian" in Cameron Nish, *The French-Canadians 1759-1766*, Copp Clark Publishing Company, Montreal, 1966.

17. Quoted by Mason Wade, in *The French-Canadians 1760-1968*, vol. 1, MacMillan, Toronto, 1968, p. 69.

CHAPTER 2

1. BINGAY, James, *History of Canada for High Schools,* Thomas Nelson and Sons, Toronto, 1934.

2. LEGER, Jules, *Textes et réflexions sur le Canada,* La Presse, Montreal, 1982, p. 77.

3. According to a survey published June 25, 1988, in the Montreal daily *Le Devoir*, 49 percent of Francophones identify themselves first as Québécois, 39 percent as French Canadians, and 11 percent as Canadians.

CHAPTER 3

1. Pertaining to this subject, see A. I. Silver, *The French-Canadian Idea of Confederation,* University of Toronto Press, Toronto, 1982.

CHAPTER 5

1. The qualifiers "good English" and "bad English" are used essentially to differentiate between the positive and negative attitudes toward the political consequences of Quebec's specificity.

CHAPTER 6

1. FAYE, Brian, *A Guide to Jack Kerouac's Lowell,* Corporation for Celebration of Kerouac in Lowell, 1988, p. 48.

2. BARTHE, Ulric, *Wilfred Laurier on the Platform*, Turcotte/Ménard, Québec, 1890, p. 310.

3. Source: American Department of Commerce, Census Bureau, Population census of 1980: ethnic origin of the population. Quoted by Gérard J. Brault, *The French-*

Canadian Heritage in New England, McGill Queen's University Press, Montreal, 1986, p. 192.

4. See David Plante's poignant book, *The Country,* Athenaeum. New York, 1981, 160 pages.

5. See LaChapelle, Réjean and Henripin, Jacques, *La Situation-démolinguistique au Canada,* in particular Chapter 8 "Du possible au plausible", L'Institut de recherches politiques, Montreal, 1980.

6. See Tonu Parming, *The Nature of Ethnic Identity,* doctorate thesis, Yale University, 1976. This work was completed three years later by Linda Cheug Meeyan, *Modernization and Ethnicity: the Divergence Model,* doctorate thesis, Maryland University, 1979.

CHAPTER 7

1. See Fasold Ralph, *The Sociolinguistics of Society,* Basil Blackwell, Oxford, 1984, p. 213.

CHAPTER 8

1. "Nation Building" refers to an evolution of federalism in the objective of increasing federal government powers, to the detriment of provincial powers. "Province Building" is used to describe the reverse process.

2. The expression "Western Provinces" includes the four provinces to the west of Ontario, including British Columbia. The "Prairie Provinces" only include Manitoba, Saskatchewan, and Alberta.

3. On the weakening of regionalism in the Prairies, see the interesting thesis by Roger Gibbons, political analyst at the University of Calgary: *Prairie Politics and Societies: Regionalism in Decline,* Butterworths, Toronto, 1982.

4. For centuries, this "Golden Square Mile" in downtown Montreal was inhabited by a large business bourgeoisie class that was second only to London in power and wealth, in all of the British Empire.

CHAPTER 9

1. It has always been considered only natural that the country's Prime Minister be able to speak English.

CHAPTER 10

1. Constitutional experts are not unanimous on this important point.

BIBLIOGRAPHY

ALMANACH DE LA LANGUE FRANÇAISE, ACF, Montréal, 1937.

ARCHIVES PUBLIQUES DU CANADA, «Documents relatifs à la constitution du Canada, vol. 1.»

ARNOPOULOS, SHEILA MCLEOD, *Hors du Québec, point de salut?*, Libre Expression, Montréal, 1982.

ATWOOD, MARGARET, *Survival — a Thematic Guide to Canadian Literature*, Anansi, Toronto, 1972.

BALTHAZAR, LOUIS, *Bilan du nationalisme au Québec*, l'Hexagone, Montréal, 1986.

BARTHE, ULRIC, *Wilfrid Laurier on the Platform*, Turcotte/Ménard, Québec, 1890.

BERTON, PIERRE, *Why We Act Like Canadians*, Penguin Books Canada, Markham, 1987.

BINGAY, JAMES, *A History of Canada for High Schools*, Thomas Nelson and Sons, Toronto, 1934.

BEAULIEU, VICTOR-LÉVY, *Jack Kérouac*, Stanké 10-10, Montréal, 1973.

BONENFANT, JEAN-CHARLES, «L'idée du fédéralisme en 1864», in *Culture XXV*, no 4, déc. 1964.

BRAULT, GÉRARD J., *The French-Canadian Heritage in New England*, McGill-Queen's University Press, Montreal, 1986.

BERTON, RAYMOND, REITZ, JEFFREY G., VALENTINE, VICTOR, *Les frontières culturelles et la cohésion du Canada*, Institut de recherches politiques, Montréal, 1981.

BRUNET, MICHEL, *La présence anglaise et les Canadiens*, Beauchemin, Montréal, 1958.

BRUNET, MICHEL, *Les Canadiens après la Conquête, 1759-1775*, Beauchemin, Montréal, 1969.

BRYM, ROBERT J., *Regionalism in Canada*, Irwin Publishing, Toronto, 1986.

CARTER, WENDY L., "What Makes B.C. Tick: a Profile of British Columbia", Federal Bureau of Coordination of Economic Development, Vancouver, April 1985.

CHARPENTIER, LOUISE, RENÉ DUROCHER et al, *Nouvelle histoire du Québec et du Canada,* Boréal, Montréal, 1985.

CHARTERS, ANN, *Kerouac, a Biography,* Phoenix Bookshop, 1973.

CHEUNG, LINDA MEE-YAN, *Modernization and Ethnicity: the Divergence Model,* doctoral thesis, University of Maryland, 1979.

CLARK, TOM, *Jack Kerouac,* Harcourt Brace Jovanovich, New York, 1984.

CLIPPINGDALE, RICHARD, *Laurier — his Life and World,* McGraw-Hill, Toronto, 1979.

CREIGHTON, DONALD, *The Story of Canada,* Macmillan of Canada, Toronto, 1959-1971.

D'AMBOISE, LOUISE, *Résumé de la pensée politique de Laurier et de Bourassa avec une bibliographie,* travail d'étudiant effectué sous supervision, Université Laval, été 1987.

D'AMBOISE, LOUISE, *Résumé de la vie de Laurier avec une bibliographie,* travail d'étudiant effectué sous supervision, Université Laval, été 1987.

D'AMBOISE, LOUISE, *La relation Laurier-Bourassa avec une bibliographie,* travial d'étudiant effectué sous supervision, Université Laval, été 1987.

D'AMBOISE, LOUISE, *Résumé de la vie d'Honoré Mercier avec une bibliographie,* travail d'etudiant effectué sous supervision, Université Laval, été 1987.

D'AMBOISE, LOUISE, *Résumé de l'Union avec une biliographie,* travail d'étudiant effectué sous supervision, Université Laval, été 1987.

D'AMBOISE, LOUISE, *Résumé de la vie de Georges-Étienne Cartier avec une bibliographie,* travail d'étudiant effectué sous supervision, Université Laval, été 1987

D'AMOISE, LOUISE, *Bibliographie sur Louis-Hyppolite Lafontaine,* travail d'étudiant effectué sous supervision, Université Laval, été 1987.

DION, LÉON, *Québec 1945-2000, tome 1-À la recherche du Québec,* Les Presses de l'Université Laval, Québec, 1987.

DOFNY, JACQUES, *National and Ethnic Movements,* Sage Studies, Beverly Hills, 1980.

ERIKSON, ERIK H., *Enface et Société,* Delachaux et Nestlé, Neaufchatel, 1959.

ERIKSON, ERIK H., *Identity and the life cycle,* W.W. Norton, New York, 1980.

ERIKSON, ERIK H., *Luther avant Luther,* Flammarion, Paris, 1968.

FASOLD, RALPH, *The Sociolinguistics of Society*, Basil Blackwell, Oxford, 1984.

FELDMAN, ELLIOTT J., and NEVITTE (edited by), *The Future of North America: Canada, The United States and Quebec Nationalism,* Institute for Research on Public Policy, Montréal, 1979.

FISHER, JOHN, *The Afrikaners,* Cassel, London, 1969.

FOYE, BRIAN, *a Guide to Jack Kerouac's Lowell,* Corp. for Celebration of Kerouac in Lowell, 1988.

FRASER, MATTHEW, *Québec inc.,* l'Homme, Montréal, 1987.

FRÉGAULT, GUY, *La civilisation de la Nouvelle-France (1713-1744)*, Fides, Montréal, 1944.

GIBBINS, ROGER, *Conflict and Unity: an Introduction to Canadian Political life*, Methuen Pubications, Toronto, 1985.

GIBBINS, ROGER, *Prairie Politics and Societies: Regionalism in Decline*, Butterworths, Toronto, 1982.

GIBBINS, ROGER, *Regionalism: Territorial Politics in Canada and the United States*, Butterworths, Toronto, 1982.

GIBBINS, ROGER, *Senate Reform: Moving Toward the Slippery Rope*, Institute of Intergovernmental Relations, Queen's University, Kingston, 1983.

GOODENOUGH, WARD H., *Language and Society*, Benjamin/Cummings Publishing Co., Menlo Park, 1981.

GRANT, GEORGE, *Est-ce la fin du Canada? — lamentations sur l'échec du nationalisme canadien*, Hurtubise HMH, Montréal, 1987.

GROULX, LIONEL, *Histoire du Canada français*, tome 2, Fides, Montréal, 1960.

GROULX, LIONEL, *Lendemains de conquête*, Stanké, Montréal, 1977.

GWYN, RICHARD, *Trudeau, the Northern Magus*, McClelland & Stewart Ltd, Markham, 1981.

HAMEL, MARCEL-PIERRE, *Le rapport Durham*, Éditions de Québec, Montréal, 1948.

HARTZ, LOUIS, *The Founding of New Societies*, Harcourt, Brace & World, New York, 1964. In particular, chap. 7, by Kenneth McRae, "the Structure of Canadian History."

HODGE, CARL CANANAGH, "Canadian Regionalism or Canadian Federalism," in *Occasional Papers* no. 10, Department of Political Science, Carleton University, Ottawa, 1984.

HOFFET, FREDERIC, *Psychanalyse de l'Alsace*, Alsatis Colmar, 1973.

QUEEN'S PRINTER, *Preliminary Report of the Commission on Bilingualism and Biculturalism*, Ottawa, 1965.

LACHAPELLE, RÉJEAN et HENRIPIN, JACQUES, *La situation démolinguistique au Canada*, l'Institut de recherches politiques, Montréal, 1980.

LACOUTURE, JEAN, *De Gaulle*, tome 3-*Le Souverain*, Le Seuil, Paris, 1986.

LAMBERT, W.E., «Qui sont-ils ces Canadiens?», in *Psychologie canadienne*, Montréal, octobre 1970, vol. 11, no. 4.

LANDRY, LOUIS, *...Et l'assimilation, pourquoi pas?* Les Presses libres, Ottawa, 1969.

LAROSE, JEAN, *La petite noirceur*, Boréal, Montréal, 1987.

LÉGER, JULES, *Textes et réflexions sur le Canada*, La Presse, Montréal, 1982.

LÉVESQUE, RENÉ, *Attendez que je me rappelle...*, Québec-Amérique, Montréal, 1986.

LIBERSON, STANLEY, *Language and Ethnic Relations in Canada,* John Wiley, New York, 1970.

LINTEAU, DUROCHER et al., *Le Québec depuis 1930,* Boréal, Montréal, 1986.

MALONE, MARC, *Une place pour le Québec au Canada,* Institut de recherches politiques, Montréal, 1986.

MIQUELON, DALE, *Society and Conquest: the Debate on the Bourgeoisie and Social Change in French Canada 1700-1850,* Copp Clark, Montréal, 1977.

MAHEU, ROBERT, *Les francophones du Canada 1941-1991,* Les éditions Parti pris, Montréal, 1970.

MONIÈRE, DENIS, *Le développement des idéologies au Québec, des origines à nos jours,* Québec-Amérique, Ottawa, 1977.

MORIN, CLAUDE, *Lendemains piégés — du référendum à la nuit des longs couteaux,* Boréal, Montréal, 1988.

MORIN, EDGAR, *Sociologie,* Fayard, Paris, 1984.

NISH, CAMERON, "1760-1770", in *Colonists and Canadiens, 1760-1867.* J.M.S. Careless, Macmillan, Toronto, 1971.

NISH, CAMERON, (collection of texts by different authors); *The French-Canadians 1759-1766. Conquered? Half-Conquered? Liberated?,* Copp Clark Publishing Co., Montreal, 1966.

O'SULLIVAN-SEA, KATHERINE, *Toward a Theory of Ethnic Nationalism: a comparison of Northern Ireland and Quebec,* doctoral thesis, University of Chicago, 1976.

PARMING, TONU, *The Nature of Ethnic Identity: the French-Canadians in Woonsocket,* doctoral thesis, Yale University, 1976.

PLANTE, DAVID, *The Country,* Atheneum, New York, 1981.

POLLARD, G. BRUCE, *Managing the Interface: Intergovernmental Affairs Agencies in Canada.* Institute of Intergovernmental Relations, Queen's University, Kingston, 1986.

RUMILLY, ROBERT, *Papineau,* Flammarion, Paris, 1934.

RUMILLY, ROBERT, *Histoire de la province de Québec,* tome 1 — *Georges-Étienne Cartier,* Valiquette, Montréal, 1940.

SILVER, A.I., *The French-Canadian Idea of Confederation,* University of Toronto Press, Toronto, 1982.

SIMÉON, RICHARD, *Confrontation et collaboration — les relations inter-gouvernmentales au Canada aujourd'hui,* L'Instiut d'administration publique du Canada, Toronto, 1979.

SIMÉON, RICHARD, *Les relations intergouvernmentales,* MacDonald Commission, vol. 63, Ottawa, 1986.

SYMONS, L. GLADYS, "Ideology and Social Change: Meech Lake and National Identity", revised version of a speech given in Vancouver, January 7-8, 1988.

SMILEY, D.V., *The Federal Condition in Canada,* McGraw-Hill Ryerson, Toronto, 1987.

STEWART, WALTER, *True Blue/the Loyalist Legend,* Collins, Don Mills. 1985.

TREMBLAY, MARC-ADÉLARD, *L'identité québécoise en péril,* Saint-Yves inc., Sainte-Foy, 1983.

TRUDEAU, PIERRE ELLIOTT, *Le fédéralisme et la société canadienne-française,* HMH, Montréal, 1967.

WADE, MASON, *The French Canadians, 1760-1911,* vol. 1, Macmillan, Toronto, 1968.

WALLACE, BROWN/HEREWARD, SENIOR, *Victorious in Defeat: the Loyalists in Canada,* Methuen, Toronto, 1984.

WALLOT, J.-P., *Un Québec qui bougeait,* trame socio-politique du XIXe sièle, Boréal Express, Montréal, 1973.

WEBER, MAX, *Le savant et le politique,* Paris, Plon, 1959.

WEINMANN, HEINZ, *Du Canada au Québec — généalogie d'une histoire,* l'Hexagone, Montréal, 1987.

The Institute for Research on Public Policy
L'Institut de recherches politique

A national, independent, research organization
Un organisme de recherche national et indépendant

Founded in 1972, The Institute for Research on Public Policy is a national organization whose independence and autonomy are ensured by the revenues of an endowment fund which is supported by the federal and provincial governments and by the private sector. In addition, the Institute receives grants and contracts from governments, corporations and foundations to carry our specific research projects.

The *raison d'être* of the Institute is threefold:

• To act as a catalyst within the national community by helping to facilitate informed public debate on issues of major public interest.
• To stimulate participation by all segments of the national community in the process that leads to public policy making.
• To find practical solutions to important public policy problems, thus aiding in the development of sound public policies.

The Institute is governed by a Board of Directors, which is the decision-making body, and a Council of Trustees, which advises the Board on matters related to the research direction of the Institute. Day-to-day administration of the Institute's policies, programs and staff is the responsibility of the president.

The Institute operates in a decentralized way, employing researchers located across Canada. This ensures that research undertaken will include contributions from all regions of the country.

Wherever possible, the Institute will try to promote public understanding of, and discussion on, issues of national importance with clarity and impartiality. Conclusions or recommendations in the Institute's publications are solely those of the author and should not be attributed to the Board of Directors, Council of Trustees, or contributors to the Institute.

The president bears final responsibility for the decision to publish a manuscript under the Institute's imprint. In reaching this decision, he is advised on the accuracy and objectivity of a mauscript by both Institute staff and outside reviewers. Publication of a manuscript signifies that it is deemed to be a competent treatment of a subject worthy of public consideration.

Publications of the Institute are published in the language of the author, along with an executive summary in both of Canada's official languages.

The Institute for Research on Public Policy
L'Institut de recherches politique

A national, independent, research organization
Un organisme de recherche national et indépendant

Créé en 1972, l'Institut de recherches politiques est un organisme national dont l'indépendance et l'autonomie sont assurés grâce a des revenus provenant d'un fonds de dotation auquel souscrivent les gouvernements fédéral et provinciaux ainisi que le secteur privé. L'Institut obient en outre des subventions et des contrats de gouvernements, des compagnies et des foundations afin de réaliser certians projets de recherche.

La raison d'être de l'Institut est triple:

• Servir de catalyseur au sein de la collectivité nationale en favorisant un débat public éclairé sur les principales questions d'intérêt général.
• Stimuler la participation de tous les éléments de la collectivité nationale à l'élaboration de la politique d'État.
• Trouver des solutions réalisables aux importants problèmes d'ordre politique afin de contribuer à l'élaboration d'une saine politique d'État.

Un Conseil d'administration, chargé de la décision, et une Commission de direction, responsable d'éclairer le Conseil sur l'orientation de la recherche, assurent la direction de l'Institut. L'administration courante des politiques, des programmes et du personnel relève du président.

L'Institut fonctionne de manière décentralisée et retient les services de chercheurs en divers points du Canada, s'assurant ainsi que toutes les régions contribuent aux recherches.

L'Institut cherche à favoriser, dans la mesure du possilbe, la compréhension et la discussion publiques des questions d'envergure nationale, controversées ou non. Il publie les conclusions de ses recherches avec clarté et impartialité. Les recommandations ou les conclusions énoncées dans les publications de l'Institut sont strictement celles de l'auteur et n'engagent aucunement le conseil d'administration, la commission de direction ou les bailleurs de fonds.

Le président assume la responsabilité ultime de publier un manuscrit au nom de l'Institut. Il jouit à cette fin des conseils du personnel de l'Institut et de critiques de l'extérieur quant à l'exactitude et l'objectivité du texte. Ne sont publiés que les textes qui traitent de façon compétente d'un sujet digne de la réflexion du public.

Les publications de l'Institut paraissent dans la langue de l'auteur et sont accompagnées d'un abrégé dans les langues officielles du Canada.